*Alternative Wedding
Ceremonies and Rituals*

Alternative Wedding Ceremonies and Rituals

Sheryle Pettifer

Alternative Wedding Ceremonies & Rituals

© 2008–2015 Sheryle Pettifer

All rights reserved by the copyright holder, Sheryle Pettifer. This book or any portion thereof may not be reproduced or transmitted in any manner whatsoever without the express written permission of the publisher.

Disclaimer

This book is designed to provide information on wedding wording only. Every effort has been made to make this book as accurate as possible and to acknowledge authors of source material. Content is not meant to be harmful, malicious, or insensitive to any individual or group. This book should serve only as a general guide. The author and publisher shall have no liability or responsibility to any person or entity regarding any loss or damage incurred, or alleged to have incurred, directly or indirectly, by the information contained in this book.

There have been many poems written about love. People have tried to describe its qualities for eons, but the best description of love was written over 12000 years ago and is found in Corinthians.

Interior layout by Mrlasers.com

Also by Sheryle Pettifer

Blessings, Readings & Vows for Weddings

Dedication

This book is dedicated **with love** to my children Reshelle Borg, Keaton Phoenix , Lee Phoenix and my three gorgeous grandsons, Jesse, Bailey and Jett. **Wishing you happiness and a life of infinite possibilies.**

Learning from each other is at the heart of a marriage. Its one of the best ways we have of connecting. It's the basis of sharing our lives together.

Dr. Markman

Contents

DEDICATION 5

INTRODUCTION 1

CULTURAL CEREMONY RITUALS 3

ALTERNATIVE CEREMONIES 5

    BABY NAMING CEREMONY CANDLE   7
    BEACH CEREMONY   18
    BLENDED FAMILY CEREMONY   20
    BLESSING OF THE ELEMENTS   22
    BLESSING OF THE ELEMENTS   26
    BLESSING OF THE ELEMENTS   30
    BLESSING OF THE HANDS   31
    BLESSING OF THE RINGS CEREMONY   33

CEREMONIES 37

    BREAKING THE GLASS CEREMONY   38
    BUDDHIST CEREMONY   43
    BURNING BOWL CEREMONY   46
    BUTTERFLY RELEASE   48
    CANDLE LIGHTING UNITY CEREMONY   51
    CELTIC RING WARMING   58
    CHILDRENS CANDLE   60
    CHILDREN IN THE CEREMONY   61
    CHRISTIAN CEREMONY   64
    COMMITMENT CEREMONY   66
    COIN OR ARRAS CEREMONY   68
    DOVE RELEASE   70
    FAMILY BLESSINGS   76
    FAMILY MEDALLION   78
    FAMILY UNITY CANDLE CEREMONY – CHILDREN   80
    FAMILY VOWS BLENDING   80
    GIVING AWAY THE BRIDE   82

Giving flowers to mothers of the bride and groom	84
Hand fasting	88
Jumping the broom	108
Knot tying ceremony	111
Love letter ceremony	114
Marriage bell	119
Memory candle	121
Oathing stone	123
Rose ceremony	126
Medieval ceremony	134
Ribbon Ceremony	135
Ring warming ceremony	136
Rose ceremony	139
Same sex ceremony	144
Sand ceremony	148
Sharing first drink as husband and wife	163
Stone ceremony	164
Sweeping the broom	164
Traditional ceremony	165
Tree circle (cairn)	166
Tree planting ceremony	166
Tying of the knot	169
Unity bowl ritual	173
Vow with children	175
Warming of the rings	176
Wedding customs from around the world	177
Wine – sharing of wine (quaich)	178
With us in spirit	187
Wearing the kilt/tartan	190

Introduction

Traditions helped define who people are and provide something stable and reliable to make them feel safe and protected. Some grew from superstition and were felt to ward off negative spirits or encourage good luck.

Like most other social institutions, marriage as we know it today evolved over centuries. The union has increased in complexity as societies have become more sophisticated and civilised. Steeped in custom and tradition, religion and civil law, many practices have gradually been adapted, adjusted or disappeared completely and new ones have replaced them. Many ceremonies have been adapted and evolved to suit the times. There is no historical purity that we can be certain of. Therefore feel free to adapt a tradition or ritual that you like to suit your own style or taste.

Your ceremony can have a theme depending on your beliefs or tastes.

The creative style of your wedding ceremony can set the tone for the rest of the ceremony.

I hope you find within this book something of interest for your ceremony. Wishing you blessings and happiness.

Cultural Ceremony Rituals

Every culture has traditional marriage rituals. Most wedding customs or rituals have their roots and popularity based on historical significance, or ethnic origin. They were often based on folklore, religion, symbolism, superstition or uniquely designed for a wedding. The exact origin and usefulness of some ceremony rituals is not clear. Many have been kept because of the historical or ethnic factor. They are certainly entertaining, colourful and enjoyable.

There are so many traditions, customs and folklores to draw upon. There are many wedding traditions, or rituals that you may like to incorporate into your ceremony to celebrate your heritage. Remember wedding customs are echoes of the past and historical accuracy is difficult to achieve. Over time rituals have been lost, embellished and designed, so do not be afraid to include an individual element of your own tastes and style to add elegance to the ceremony.

There are also books available and information on the internet to help you in designing a custom ceremony.

Included are some examples of alternative ceremonies, rituals and symbols that can be incorporated into your service. Where you find the words Bride and Groom, this would be replaced with the names of the Bride and Groom. The work in this book is an example only. You can add, omit, adjust, etc. to suit your individual tastes. Enjoy!

Alternative Ceremonies

BABY NAMING CEREMONY CANDLE

A naming ceremony is a non-religious way of welcoming the birth of a child and officially introducing him/her to your family and friends. Naming ceremonies are appropriate for anyone, at any age and can be a way of celebrating a new step-family, adopted children, or an adult name change.

A baby naming ceremony can also be part of the wedding ceremony, a special candle, with the baby's name, date of birth and/or photograph can be part of the candle lighting ceremony. Some of the other ceremony examples can be included if you desire like the sand ceremony.

An example of a Baby Naming Ceremony/Candle can be as follows:

Welcome Introduction
Poem/Reading
Recognition of siblings
Naming of Baby
Parents Promises
Acknowledgement and appointment of the Godparents/
    Guardians
Welcoming Child to the Family and your friends
Declaration of love and ongoing support
Poem or blessing
Signing of the Commemorative Naming Certificate by all
    parties
Presentation of the Certificate and Closing Words
Presentation of baby for congratulations and photos!

Ceremony 1

Welcome family and friends to today's ceremony. This is an auspicious occasion, the naming of a child and their formal welcoming into the circle of family and friends. Mother and Father (names) are overjoyed at his/her safe arrival into this world, Today (Mother) and (Father) have invited us to take part in this ceremony to express their commitment to their baby and his/her future.

The birth of a child is a most joyous occasion. A celebration of the miracle of life. In welcoming and naming a child with this ceremony, we celebrate one of life's miracles.

The responsibility of a child's life and their wellbeing is the obligation of not only the child's parents, but the family, friends and indeed the community if we desire a child to grow into a healthy balanced individual and a credit to themselves and to society.

The world is shaped by the influence we have on our children in our homes. It is the way we treat our children that determines largely whether they will grow to be a contribution to the world or a burden.

Today we come to celebrate this child's life and to share in Mother and Fathers (names) joy. There is a most important reason that you have been invited here. Each of you is of great consequence to this child's life. It is the combination of your characteristics and qualities that form your distinctive character. Your individual personalities have value and substance. It is our personality style that propels us on our life path. It represents all of our attributes, thoughts, feelings, attitudes, behaviours, and coping mechanisms. The positive strength of these attributes is of intrinsic value to the happiness and success of not only our life but all who share our life. You stand here today because it is your value to this family and your personality style that complements the family and will offer constructive substance to this baby's life.

Reading

We gather today to bless a child. A new life that has become part of our world. We gather today to name this child. To call a thing by name is to give it power, and so today we shall give this child a gift. We will welcome her into our hearts and lives and bless her with a name of her own.

Promise/Pledge

Mother and Father. Do you promise to give this child your unconditional love and support? Will you do your utmost share a healthy and loving relationship that someday she/he may replicate the same?

Parents: We will.

The Naming

A name is very important as it distinguishes us from others and gives us a sense of belonging in our family and community.

Mother and Father, may I please have the chosen name you have given this child? Let us name this child. Together with me place a hand on the head of your child and say:

We name you *Child's full name.*

SIGNIFICANCE OF THE CHOSEN NAME OR REASON THE NAME WAS CHOSEN.

E.g. the name Anne is a Hebrew baby name. In Hebrew the meaning of the name Anne is: **favour or grace.**

APPOINTED GODPARENTS/GUARDIANS/ SPONSORS/MENTORS COMMITMENT OFFERED TO THE CHILD.

I now ask the mentors: Do you solemnly swear to take a special and lifelong interest in (baby's name) welfare and offer you friendship, counsel, and support in their life?—We do

PROMISES BY LIFE GUARDIANS

Mother and Father have asked Names to be guardians to Child. Please can they join us at the front?

(POEM COULD BE INCLUDED HERE, READ BY A CHOSEN READER)

The bond between parents and their children is very strong, but the support and encouragement of others is vital for the development of a child.

It is for this reason that Life Guardians are chosen. Someone willing to take a special and lifelong interest in the moral and ethical development of this child. To be there for additional support. Someone they can turn to for guidance or to offer assistance.

Life Guardians, as you accept the role of a Life Guardian, you are agreeing to be an adult friend to Child's name. Someone to whom he/she can turn for loving support and guidance. Will you accept this commitment and responsibility?

Life Guardians: I will.

Promises by Grandparents

Father and Mother acknowledge the special relationship between Baby and her Grandparents.

Grandparents play an extremely important and active role in the life of a child. It is through the relating of their life experiences, their stories of people, places and events they have known that children develop and learn family history, social skills, and life values.

Grandparents, I ask you now. Will you lovingly support Child's name. Providing a safe and loving refuge? Offering counsel whenever requested and supporting her/his potential to the best of your ability.

Grandparents: I will.

Blessing for the Child

Wishing you many smiles and happy times to come by Anon (adjusted)

May life's adventures be exciting and sweet. Filled with love from the friends that you'll meet. You'll soon grow up for time does fly, may you cherish each moment as it goes by, from crawling and walking to toddling and talking.

There's no knowing what you'll do next

There's a threshold to cross and a wide open door and a wonderful world for you to explore. Sleep with the moonbeams and play in the sun. May your life be a long one and filled with promise and fun. May today and tomorrow and all days hereafter be days that are blissful and filled with your laughter.

OR

May beauty delight you and happiness uplift you.

May wonder fulfil you and love surround you.

May your step be steady and your arm be strong.

May your heart be peaceful and your word be true.

May you seek to learn, may you learn to live.

May you live to love, and may you love always.

Irish Baby Blessing

May all the blessings of our Lord touch your life today.

May he send his little angels to protect you on your way.

Such a miraculous gift, sent from above.

Someone so precious to cherish and love.

May sunshine and moonbeams dance over your head.

as you quietly slumber in your bed.

May good luck be with you wherever you go.

and your blessings outnumber the shamrocks that grow.

OR

TRADITIONAL IRISH BLESSING

May you always have walls for the winds.

A roof for the rain, tea beside the fire.

Laughter to cheer you, those you love near you,

and all your heart might desire.

May the sun shine all day long, everything go right, and nothing wrong.

May those you love bring love back to you and may all the wishes you wish come true. May luck be your friend in whatever you do and may trouble be always

a stranger to you.

POEM OR READING

I will now read a poem that has been especially chosen:

A PARENT'S WISH BY ANON (ADJUSTED FROM A MOTHERS WISH)

We hope our child looks back on today and sees parents who had time to play.

There will be years for cleaning and cooking, but children grow up when you're not looking.

Tomorrow we'll do all the chores you can mention, but today, our baby needs time and attention.

So settle down cobwebs; dust go to sleep.

We're cuddling our baby, and babies don't keep.

The Example of Parenthood

There are little eyes upon you and they're watching night and day.

There are little ears that quickly take in everything you say.

There are little hands all eager to do everything you do

and a little girl/boy who's dreaming of the day she'll be like you.

You're little Childs name idol you're the wisest of the wise.

In her little mind about you no suspicions ever rise.

There's a wide-eyed little girl/boy who believes you're always right

and her ears are always open as she watches day and night.

You are setting an example every day in all you do.

For the little girl/boy who's waiting to grow up to be like you.

Children Learn what they Live by Dorothy Law Nolte

If children live with criticism, they learn to condemn.
If children live with hostility, they learn to fight.
If children live with fear, they learn to be apprehensive.

If children live with pity, they learn to feel sorry for themselves.
If children live with ridicule, they learn to feel shy.
If children live with jealousy, they learn to feel envy.
If children live with shame, they learn to feel guilty.
If children live with encouragement, they learn confidence.
If children live with tolerance, they learn patience.
If children live with praise, they learn appreciation.
If children live with acceptance, they learn to love.
If children live with approval, they learn to like themselves.
If children live with recognition, they learn it is good to have a goal.
If children live with sharing, they learn generosity.
If children live with honesty, they learn truthfulness.
If children live with fairness, they learn justice.
If children live with kindness and consideration, they learn respect.
If children live with security, they learn to have faith in themselves and in those about them.
If children live with friendliness, they learn the world is a nice place in which to live.

PRESENTATION OF CHILD TO FAMILY AND FRIENDS

Child's full name you have been named by your family. Guardians/mentors have been appointed. Family and friends have offered up their love and blessings. It is an honour to welcome you into this family and community.

Presentation of Naming Certificate

The parents are presented with a commemorative certificate signed by the Celebrant, the parents and the Godparents.

I now present Baby's Name, naming certificate

Certificates for any Guardians Appointed/Certificates for Grandparents

I would like to present these certificates to Guardians Names on behalf of baby and parents.

Presentation of Gifts/Tokens

Happiness doesn't result from what we get, but from what we give. These gifts are some of the first gifts you will receive in life. Your birth is a wonderful blessing and gift to us of love.

Toast

Child's full name you have been named by your family and your guardians/ mentors have been appointed.

We will drink a toast of welcome before the closing words of this ceremony.

Family and Friends to Name!

Closing Words

It is the responsibility of us all to encourage the virtues we should all aspire to, that (baby's name) will mature to have integrity as well as positive work and personal ethics.

It is the desire and wish of all present that (child's name) has every happiness in their life. (Baby's name) we wish you long life and happiness. We ask the universe to bless you so that you grow to be kind and compassionate and have the good fortune to find success in your life. It is our dearest wish you not only find true love in your life, but that you be true love.

OR

On behalf of Mother and Father, I'd like to thank you for your attendance, affirmations and support in the past, present and future. May life's richest joys and blessings be yours.

Symbolisms that can be included in the Ceremony:

Lighting Candles by Parents/Siblings/Godparents/
    Grandparents
Planting a Tree
Presentation of jewellery
Naming Candle
Butterfly Release
Time Capsule
Signature Bear

BEACH CEREMONY

OPENING

Bride and Groom want to thank all of you for sharing is this celebration of their commitment to each other. As the tides ebb and flow so to, do the fortunes of life. Footprints in the sand are washed away, driftwood moves on its endless quest for a peaceful harbour. Only a deep and abiding love can with stand the tides of change in two lives. The love of Bride and Groom is enduring and profound. We gather here to witness this love and the vows they make to each other.

VOWS

Today you join yourselves together for life as friends and lovers. Husband and Wife. As the surface of the sea is sometimes calm and often storm tossed, so also is a marriage?

Groom/Bride: I pledge to you that my love and loyalty will weather the storms of life. I will seek your counsel when I make important decisions, and will respect your needs and concerns. No matter what course we set, we will do it together.

RING CEREMONY

Bride/Groom: I give you this ring as a symbol of my commitment to you, as powerful and endless as the sea

PRONOUNCEMENT OF MARRIAGE

Bride and Groom, you have showered your hearts with expressions of your love. By the virtue of the authority vested in me it gives me great honour and pleasure to now pronounce you husband and wife. You may kiss your Bride.

BLENDED FAMILY CEREMONY

Most often we think of marriage as the joining of two people. In reality, marriage is often much more than that. It is also the coming together and merging of family and friends. When the Bride and/or Groom have children, it is appropriate for the children to be included in the wedding ceremony. With children present, the wedding ceremony also becomes the proclamation of a new family or a family wedding.

Generally speaking, children will accept a parent's remarriage more readily when they feel included in the wedding plans and the wedding ceremony and are given a tangible symbol of being embraced by a new family. Giving a gift, perhaps a beautiful bracelet, a birthstone ring or some other significant token of love with appropriate words of love and support will make them feel a special part of the ceremony. Blended families can easily be incorporated into the wedding ceremony. Pouring different coloured sands together is a way to symbolise the joining of the Bride and Groom and their family together. See the Blending of the Sands Ceremony.

Blended Family Ceremony 1

It is the desire of Bride and Groom to extend their commitments to each other by making some promises to the children of this family. Bride and Groom please join hands with the children to form a circle of love. We seal this union with spoken promises and the rings this Bride and Groom have exchanged.

Celebrant to the Bride/Groom: Do you Bride and Groom promise to be faithful, loving, tender and nurturing parents, always there for (child/children's name). Not only providing their/her/his physical needs, but their/her/his emotional needs as well. Always a good listener, a loving counsellor and friend.

Bride & Groom: We do.

Groom/Bride to children: I want you to know that I love your mother/father very much. I am not your mother/father however I promise that I do my best to care for you as if you were my own. I promise to listen to you and help you however and whenever I can. If you need help at any time I want you to feel free to ask me.

Bride/Groom to Child/Children: This gift is to seal the promises I've made to you today.

Celebrant: May the universe bless you all as family, and bless this marriage.

BLESSING OF THE ELEMENTS

Over time many Ceremonies have encompassed the theory of love and respect for nature and the belief that life is made of these elements. Ceremonies that bless the elements pay respect to the individual elements that represent North: fire, South: air, East: water or West: earth. They may encompass the love and respect of nature. Blessings, whether they're Irish or Jewish, ancient or modern, are an important part of our faith in life. The element in any blessing is that there needs to be a relationship with the universe. The senses of the wind, the rain and the sun, can convey life sustenance. Blessings, whether they're ancient or modern, are an important part of life and relationship with the universe. They are offered from the heart in the belief that they will enhance the receiver. The most important of the blessings that we can bestow in life is the blessing of love for love is a wondrous comforting gift. Everyday life presents many opportunities for blessing one another.

A blessing is the bridge between the heavens and the earth. Believing in the good. That it will enhance the receiver. It also envisions a goodness that will comfort and give hope to all. We have the ability to envision virtually any hope for ourselves, for humanity. In our society of abundance, if we are the lucky ones who have, we take much for granted. Perhaps the most important of the blessings that we can bestow in life is the blessing of love for love is a wondrous thing.

Today we are calling a blessing upon this marriage

Herbs or incense can be burned to burn away negative energies or influences. Incense can heighten our senses, lift our spirits and sooth our souls. Couples can stand in a circle than has been drawn or made with flowers etc. before the ceremony. This becomes a sacred circle. There are many variations of blessing of the elements ceremonies. Perhaps add your own touch.

CEREMONY OF THE ELEMENTS 1

Today we are calling a blessing from nature in respect of the individual elements representing the North: fire, South: air, East: water or West: earth. We bless this marriage in the desire that it thrives. The wind, the rain, the sun, the waters convey life sustenance.

In many cultures it is believed that the human soul shares characteristics with all things divine. I now respectfully call upon the four cardinal directions, East, South, West and North to bless this marriage.

Bride and Groom each of these blessings from the four cardinal directions emphasises those things which can help you build a happy and successful marriage.

May your marriage be blessed with the gifts of the East: Air/Spring

Imagination and new beginnings

May you have communication of the heart and purity of the mind and body. From the East you receive new beginnings. With the rising of each sun there is a new day with opportunity for growth.

Air is an element of the East: It is the breath of life. The power of air can breathe new life into us. It is an element that enables co-existence of the two main elements, fire and water. We call on the power of the East. The power of life, opportunity and co-existence.

May your marriage be blessed with the gifts of the South: Fire/Summer

Passion and Excitement

May you find passion, creativity and the warmth of a loving home.

Fire is an element of the South: A purifying energy. Fire brings about new life and razes the old. It transforms and makes new. May it warm you through the cold of winter and light your way in darkness. We call on the power of the South, the warmth, and love.

May your marriage be blessed with the gifts of the West: Water/Autumn

Emotions and Intuition.

Water is an element of the West. Life giving, soothing, healing, cleansing and renewing. Its power is strong and shaping, as water shapes a stone. We call on the power of the West fortifying and creative.

May your marriage be blessed with the gifts of the North: Earth/Winter

Steadfastness and courage.

Earth is the element of the North. The Earth is nurturing. It provides sustenance to feed, clothe and shelter. We call on the power of the North the comforting and nourishment.

BLESSING OF THE ELEMENTS

We invoke the four elements:

> *Light and radiance of the Sun*
> *Warmth and renewal of Fire*
> *Energy of the Wind*
> *Inner depth of the Sea*
> *Stability and sustainability of Earth*
> *I call upon thee, please bless my path*
> *So shall it be!*

These are the horoscope signs by the elements:

Fire	Aries, Leo, and Sagittarius
Earth	Taurus, Virgo, Capricorn
Air	Gemini, Libra, Aquarius
Water	Cancer, Scorpio, Pisces

May the breath of life bear witness to this ritual and the winds carry this message to all lands. May the sun, warm these hearts, and fire fuel their desire for each other. May the waters provide for them from their bounty, and comfort their souls with her sounds. May the earth lend its strength, and reveal its mysteries.

Ceremony of the Elements 2

All gathered here today are representatives of the universe. The bond and covenant of marriage is established by positive actions, and blessed by spiritual living.

In many cultures it is believed that the human soul shares characteristics with all things divine. I now respectfully call upon the four cardinal directions, East, South, West and North.

Bride and Groom each of these blessings from the four cardinal directions emphasize those things which can help you build a happy and successful marriage.

May your marriage be blessed with the gifts of the East: Air/Spring

Imagination and new beginnings

May you have communication of the heart and purity of the mind and body. From the East you receive new beginnings. With the rising of each sun there is a new day with opportunity for growth.

Air is an element of the East: It is the breath of life. The power of air can breathe new life into us. It gives us the ability to see the dawn. It gives us the power of the wind. We call on the power of the East. The power of life and opportunities.

May your marriage be blessed with the gifts of the South: Fire/Summer

Passion and Excitement

May you find passion, creativity and the warmth of a loving home.

Fire is an element of the South: Fire is a purifying energy. It both creates and destroys, and symbolises fertility. Fire can heal or harm and can bring about new life or destroy the old. The power of fire, transforms and makes new. May it warm you through the cold winter. Light your way in darkness. We call on the power of the South, the warmth, and love.

May your marriage be blessed with the gifts of the West: Water/Autumn

Emotions and Intuition.

In your marriage offer each other absolute trust and vow to keep your hearts open in sorrow as well as joy.

Water is an element of the West. It is life giving with its rivers and oceans. Water is soothing, healing, cleansing and renewing. Its power is strong and shaping, as a river shapes a stone. We call on the power of the West the nurturing, healing and strength.

May your marriage be blessed with the gifts of the North: Earth/Winter

Steadfastness and courage.

The wedding day is just the first step and only a small part of the courageous act of marriage, for it takes courage to step into the unknown and courage and patience to stand steadfast and face any difficulties that may confront you in marriage with honesty.

Earth is the element of the North. The Earth is nurturing and stable, solid and firm, full of endurance and strength. It provides sustenance to feed, clothe and shelter. It enriches and provides so that you may build a home for your family. It also reminds us to rest in the winter for the earth needs respite from the work of growing. Therefore be at rest when you retreat to your home, so that you are renewed in body and soul. We call on the power of the North the comforting and nourishment.

BLESSING OF THE ELEMENTS

In winter, it's hard to remember sometimes that warmth is coming back to earth. However, despite the grey, cloudy days, we know that soon, the sun will return. We now invoke the four elements:

> *As the earth grows colder,*
> *the winds blow faster,*
> *the fire dwindles smaller,*
> *and the rains fall harder,*
> *let the light of the sun*
> *find its way home.*

For your information, here are the signs divided by the elements:

Fire	Aries, Leo, and Sagittarius
Earth	Taurus, Virgo, Capricorn
Air	Gemini, Libra, Aquarius
Water	Cancer, Scorpio, Pisces

May the gentle breeze bear witness to this ritual and carry its message to all lands.

May the sun, warm their hearts, and its ever-burning fire fuel their desire for each other. May the sea provide for them from its bounty, and comfort their souls with her sounds. May the earth lend its strength, and reveal its mysteries.

BLESSING OF THE HANDS

Bride, please hold Grooms hands palms up, so you may see the gift that they are to you.

These are the hands of your best friend, young and strong and vibrant with love, that are holding yours on your wedding day, as he promises to love you all the days of his life.

These are the hands that will work alongside yours, as together you build your future, as you laugh and cry, as you share your innermost secrets and dreams.

These are that hands that will passionately love you and cherish you through the years, for a lifetime of happiness.

These are the hands that will countless times wipe the tears from your eyes. Tears of sorrow and tears of joy.

These are the hands that will comfort you in illness, and hold you when fear or grief engulfs your heart. These are the hands that will tenderly lift your chin and brush your cheek, as they raise your face to look into his eyes: eyes that are filled completely with his overwhelming love and desire for you.

Groom please hold Brides, hands palms up, so you may see the gift that they are to you.

These are the hands of your best friend, smooth, young and carefree, that are holding yours on your wedding day, as she pledges her love and commitment to you all the days of her life.

These are the hands that will massage tension from you in the evenings after you've both had a long hard day. These are the hands that will hold you tight, as you struggle through difficult times. These are the hands that will comfort you when you are sick, or console you when you are grieving.

These are the hands that will passionately love you and cherish you through the years, for a lifetime of happiness.

These are the hands that will give you support as you follow your dreams. Together as a team, everything you wish for can be realised.

BLESSING OF THE RINGS CEREMONY

In the Blessing of the Rings element of the ceremony, the Celebrant says a blessing over the rings. It is also common for the Celebrant to speak of the symbolism and meaning of the rings, such as how the rings are an outward sign of the couple's commitment to one another. The unending circle of a ring symbolises faithfulness and love without end.

The wedding rings can be held by the Best Man, Maid of Honour, person of your choosing, or kept in a lovely container such as a box.

Ring Blessing 1

Bless these Rings. May they be a reminder of the promises you made today. Share peace with each other and grow old together in your love.

Ring Blessing 2

Your love is like sunshine, warming all that it touches and like the moon it will brighten your nights. In each other's arms may it always embrace you, making all right with your world.

Ring Blessing 3

Bless these rings. When you look at them may they always remind you of the vows and promises you have made today and may your hearts be loving always.

Ring Blessing 4

The rings you exchange today are a sign of your commitment and a testimony of your devotion to each other and to your marriage.

Ring Blessing 5

Bless these rings. They symbolise the spirit of your vows in marriage.

Ring Blessing 6

May these rings be eternal symbols of your commitment and affection for each other.

Ring Blessing 7

These rings are blessed as the symbol of your affectionate unity. Two lives joined as one. Wherever you go, may you always return to one another in togetherness.

Ring Blessing 8

Bless these rings. Grant that Bride and Groom wear them with deep faith in each other. May they always live together in peace, love and abiding joy.

Ring Blessing 9

The circle is the symbol of the sun, earth, and universe. It is the symbol of peace. Let this ring be the symbol of unity and peace in which your two lives are joined in one unbroken circle. Wherever you go, return unto one another and to your togetherness.

Ring Blessing 10

The wedding ring is a symbol of eternity. It is an outward sign of a commitment and spiritual bond which unites two hearts in endless love.

Ring Blessing 11

The circle of the ring declares the unity and the oneness of your two lives, which shall contain your devotion that after every journey, you will always return again to your togetherness.

Ring Blessing 11

May these rings remind you that your love, like the sun, warms all that it touches, and your love like the arms that embrace you, makes everything right with the world.

Ring Blessing 12

Wear these rings as a bond of reverence and trust. Protect the love that now makes you one.

Ring Blessing 13

Bless these rings as a symbol of your affectionate unity. Two lives now joined as one. Wherever you go, may you always return to one another in togetherness. You have found in each other the love for which all men and women yearn. May it grow through understanding and compassion.

RING BLESSING 14

May the home, which you establish together, be a place of sanctuary. May these rings ring symbolise always the spirit of love in your heart.

Ceremonies

BREAKING THE GLASS CEREMONY

Breaking of the glass at the end of a wedding ceremony is symbolic of two important aspects of a marriage. The permanent and final breaking of this glass is irreversible. It is symbolic of the frailty of a marriage. That sometimes a single thoughtless act, breach of trust, or infidelity can damage a marriage in irreversible ways. Bride and Groom strive always to show each other love and understanding. In doing this you will feel secure and your vows, your love and your marriage will be unbreakable.

The "glass" is usually a light bulb wrapped in a white napkin or towel. Sometimes a wine glass is difficult to break. The best man hands the minister the glass. The minister will say a few words to explain the significance of the breaking of the glass. He then places the glass on the ground before the Groom.

After the Celebrant declares the Bride and Groom to be husband and wife he/she invites the couple to seal their promises with a kiss. The Groom kisses the Bride and then breaks the glass with his right foot. Some couples choose to break the glass together. The breaking of the glass is usually after the exchanging of rings and just before declaring the couple to be husband and wife.

In Greece, the custom of breaking plates during the reception symbolises good luck, happiness and the permanence of marriage.

It is also symbolic that once the glass is shattered, it can never return to its former state. It also reflects the breaking down of barriers to build a relationship of respect, unity and peace.

Just as this glass can be shattered with a single blow, so the grace of your marriage bond can be shattered with an act of irresponsibility.

The Celebrant holds the covered glass while reading the following:

Breaking the Glass 1

There have been many stories explaining the breaking of the glass. It serves to remind us of several very important aspects of a marriage. That marriage vows are precious, just as this glass is precious and without care can be shattered.

Breaking the Glass 2

We conclude this ceremony with the Breaking of the Glass. The breaking of a glass serves as a reminder of the sanctity of marriage and how precious should be its care.

Breaking the Glass 3

The shattering of glass reminds us how fragile life and love can be. That sometimes a thoughtless act can damage a marriage irrevocably just as breaking of glass is irreparable.

BREAKING THE GLASS 4

In Jewish tradition, the Breaking of the Glass at a wedding is a symbolic prayer and hope that your love for one another will remain until the pieces of the glass come together again, or in other words, that your love will last forever. The fragile nature of the glass also suggests the frailty of human relationships. Even the strongest of relationships is subject to disintegration. The glass then, is broken to protect the marriage with the prayer, "May your bond of love be as difficult to break as it would be to put together the pieces of this glass."

(The Groom then stomps on the glass with his foot and everyone shouts "Mazel Tov"! which means "Good Luck and Congratulations, or they can shout Good Luck and Congratulations!

BREAKING THE GLASS 5

Symbolically, the breaking of the glass reminds us of the fragile nature of life. The custom has also come to symbolise the shattering of the old and the beginning of the new. The breaking of the glass insures the uniqueness of the moment that arises and passes away, a letting go of the past and looking toward the future.

Since this is an interfaith ceremony, that brings two people from different religious and cultural backgrounds together, this symbol becomes especially mindful of the barriers that people erect between one another. The breaking of the glass is symbolic of a breaking down of the barriers between people which will help create a world based on love, unity, peace, and understanding. The breaking of the glass represents a turning point in your lives as you pledge your love today and make vows of commitment to one another.

Breaking the Glass 6

The final act of this ceremony is the shattering of the glass. This old custom has many traditions, and interpretations. Today, the fragility of the glass suggests the frailty of human relationships. It also represents the end of your lives as individuals because you are now facing the future as one united in life and love.

Breaking the Glass 7

Bride and Groom, this glass symbolises the clarity of your love for each other and the shattering of your separate lives so that you begin from this moment on as a couple. As you break the glass, our blessings will be bestowed upon you. 'Congratulations.'

Breaking the Glass 8

This glass is a beautiful thing, as is a considerate and loving marriage. If cared for properly, it can last a lifetime. Like a marriage though, it can also be frail and careful consideration must be given to its life just if you want it to last a lifetime.

At the end of the Ceremony before the Breaking:

CELEBRANT

In a moment, Groom will break the glass signifying the fragility of marriage and the importance of treating your relationship with tender care. It will also signify the end of the ceremony and the time for celebration.

Celebrant places the covered glass on the floor and after the couple is declared to be wife and husband, and the Groom kisses the Bride, the Groom steps on the glass with his right foot.

Ladies and Gentlemen, it is my pleasure to introduce to you, Mr. & Mrs.

Now, go in peace and forever Celebrate Love!

BUDDHIST CEREMONY

The Buddhist belief is that the couple make a pledge to a greater truth. Buddhism allows each couple to decide for themselves all the issues pertaining to marriage.

The couple together can create their own marriage vows and promises and make a pledge to a greater truth rather than to each other, based on Buddhist scriptures.

BUDDHIST CEREMONY 1

Bride and Groom you place your hearts into each other's keeping today.

Fulfil your friendship and express your gratitude to life for the gift of love and each other. This is truly a great and joyous occasion for you have chosen to share your lives together wholeheartedly. Nothing happens without cause. Be the hearts innermost quest and practice loving kindness. Marriage is a lifelong

commitment. Act with generosity and kindness. Be consciously loving with honour and truth. Speak with integrity from the depth of your hearts. Act with mindfulness and consideration.

Remember the preciousness of silence. Rejoice in your good fortune and be sympathetic of misfortune. Do not through thoughts, words or actions, separate yourselves from each other through coveting, envy or jealousy. Act to the best of your ability with calm, compassion and loving kindness.

(Ring Bell/s)

You are married heart to heart, mind to mind, body to body, nature to nature. Today you give up your single self to take loving refuge in each other. In marriage share a living spiritual practice together. Remember your marriage is a sacred and blessed undertaking, witnessed by all.

Purify with incense

(Ring Bell/s)

Exchange of Rings

(Ring Bell/s)

Pronouncement

After witnessing that you have exchanged vows, according to the wisdom of Buddha and by the rights vested in me, I joyously pronounce you Husband and Wife.

BUDDHIST CEREMONY 2

OPENING WORDS

Traditional Buddhist prayer

Today you promise to dedicate yourselves completely to each other with body, speech, and mind. In this life, in every situation, wealth or poverty, health or sickness, happiness or difficulty, strive to help each other.

The purpose of your relationship will be to attain enlightenment by perfecting your kindness and compassion toward all sentient beings.

Vows

Do you pledge to help each other to develop your hearts and minds? Cultivating compassion, generosity, ethics, patience, enthusiasm and wisdom.

Rings

The wedding ring is the outward and visible sign of an inward and spiritual bond which unites two loyal hearts in partnership. We have come together in your presence to celebrate and bless the joining together of Bride and Groom.

A spiritual life is a path of transformation of one's inner potential. A path dedicated to serving others in awakening their potential. Marriage is a vehicle for the practice of serving others.

Love is the desire to share happiness and growth. It is a commitment to the happiness and wellbeing of your partner. All gathered here today are representatives of the universe. The bond and covenant of marriage is established by positive actions, and blessed by spiritual living. Bride and Groom vow to dedicate their marriage to the wellbeing of all living beings.

BURNING BOWL CEREMONY

The Ancients burned incense in ceremonies to celebrate life and to generate prosperity, longevity, happiness and love. In today's ceremony the Bride and Groom have chosen to honour this tradition by the lighting of incense to celebrate life and new beginnings.

Paracelsus an ancient philosopher said. "Truly it has been said that there is nothing new under the sun, for knowledge is revealed and is submerged again". The Ancients burned incense in ceremonies to celebrate life and to generate prosperity, longevity, happiness, and love. In today's ceremony the Bride and Groom have chosen to honour this tradition by the lighting of incense (in a bowl with sides) to celebrate life and new beginnings

The Burning Bowl Ceremony has also been altered somewhat to where a letter is burnt. This is a fire ceremony designed to help a couple listen, become clear in their positive intentions, release old habits that get in the way of those intentions, and bring in new habits that can help them accomplish their good intentions.

The bowl used is a metal vessel. It is mounted on a wrought iron stand. The flame is provided by a pillar candle. The papers can be held over the flame with tongs.

The couple hold the paper over a burning flame and release it into the Universal Energy to be cleansed. The ashes can later if wished be spread on the earth to fertilise the soil for new life.

The Burning Bowl Ceremony can be a ceremony where a couple write on pieces of paper that which they wish released from their past, so that they move cleansed into their marriage. In my ceremonies I have the couple write only positive intentions on the pieces of paper so that they start off with their minds and hearts full of positive intent.

WORDING EXAMPLE

Bride and Groom have focused their attention on what they would like created in their life and marriage by writing those intentions on paper. They will now burn the paper/s sending their prayers to the Creator/Universe. The Burning Bowl ceremony invites the conscious loving universe to this ceremony to assist you in your marriage.

Bride and Groom your hearts are like this fire warm and glowing with your love. In your marriage if you face any unpleasant feelings with care, affection, and calm, you will transform them into positive energy that is healthy and has the capacity to nourish your marriage. With all the forces of the universe we pray for harmony and true happiness to fill your hearts and souls.

OR

These messages rise from the warmth of two hearts into the heavens. Bride and Grooms lives and spirits are joined in a union of love and trust today. May the intensity of their love burn with inner strength to be refined to gold.

We ask for blessings upon this Ceremony and Marriage.

BUTTERFLY RELEASE

WORDING FOR RELEASE OF BUTTERFLIES

WORDING 1

If anyone desires a wish to come true they must first capture a butterfly and whisper that wish to it. Since a butterfly can make no sound, the butterfly cannot reveal the wish to anyone but the Universe who hears and sees all. In gratitude for giving the beautiful butterfly its freedom, the Universe grants the wish.

According to legend, by making a wish and giving the butterfly its freedom, the wish will be taken to the heavens and be granted. We have gathered to grant Bride and Groom our best wishes as they set these butterflies free in trust that all these wishes will be granted.

WORDING 2

Love is like a butterfly, as soft and gentle as a sigh. The multi coloured moods of love are like its satin wings. Love makes your heart feel strange inside. It flutters like soft wings in flight. Love is like a butterfly, a rare and gentle thing. I feel it when you're with me. It happens when you kiss me. That rare and gentle feeling that I feel inside. Your touch is soft and gentle. Your kiss is warm and tender. Whenever I am with you, I think of butterflies. Your laughter brings me sunshine. Every day is springtime and I am only happy when you are by my side. How precious is this love we share? How very precious sweet and rare. Together we belong like daffodils and butterflies.

The release of butterflies is symbolic of new beginnings. Good fortune and joy. It is believed if you whisper your wish to a butterfly your wish will come

WINGS

You have given me wings with which to fly.
Now I breathe in deep and spread them wide
as we lift off from the silken petals
into the wind where the butterflies glide.

How many butterflies do you need?

This depends on your preference and budget. A 'special wish' symbolic release is where two individual butterflies are released by the Bride & Groom, or an individual butterfly can be released by the Bride and Groom's parents, or by each family member. You can also have a mass release of butterflies.

When should I order?

Normally a minimum of 6 weeks' notice is required for breeding purposes. As breeding schedules do book out, it is recommended that you order as early as possible to avoid disappointment. Note: Availability of butterflies is seasonal.

As butterflies are cold blooded they may not be available for releasing during the colder winter months. Check on the website regarding delivery to your area. Consider the welfare of the butterflies. It is usually policy that butterflies will not be left at an unattended address.

As butterflies are cold-blooded packaging is especially designed to keep them cool and dark. The butterflies then go into a natural hibernation type sleep. When individual butterfly release triangles are distributed to guests, the butterflies begin to warm up. This wakes them up and they will be ready to fly at the time of release. Whilst in transit, as the butterflies are sleeping they are in a reduced metabolic state and are not stressed, or harmed in any way. Check weather conditions required to release butterflies and discuss release instructions.

CANDLE LIGHTING UNITY CEREMONY

The unity candle symbolises the essence of the wedding ceremony. Lighting a Unity Candle during your wedding ceremony is a special way to symbolise your two lives joining together as one.

The ceremony is the lighting of candles to symbolise the joining of two families. . The outside taper candles represent the families of the bride and groom, and the larger center pillar candle represents the new family formed by the marriage.

There are many variations on this ceremony and many styles of candles that can be used, but usually they are large candles or tall tapers so that they can be seen by the wedding guests.

In an outdoor ceremony, candles should be placed in a deep glass container, or in a lantern designed for outdoor lighting, to ensure that the candles are protected from the elements and the wind. Remember the matches, and also to have long matches if using deep receptacles, so that fingers don't get singed. Be aware of the safety aspect of using candles!

There are several options for lighting candles. You can have parents come forward to light the side candles as a symbol of the two families coming together as one. At this point, some couples choose to present their mothers with a rose.

The Celebrant or best man and the maid of honour can light the candles, or you may light the candles yourselves from a candle on the table.

Couples can purchase a special candle for themselves that includes their names, and the date of their wedding. The candle can then be kept to light on their wedding anniversaries.

A special song or music would be lovely to accompany the candle-lighting ceremony. A singer can perform live, or you can play a recorded version as you exchange vows.

CANDLE UNITY 1

Bride and Groom, as you light this candle of unity, you symbolise the lighting of the partnership of marriage bringing the warmth, strength and wisdom of your family's warmth for your own. Bride and Groom your flames are separate, yet they feed the same fire.

CANDLE UNITY 2

This candle you are about to light is the light of Marriage. From this day onward, may you bask in the warmth of the light of your love. May its light shine bright and steady upon your path together keeping you warm through life and beyond.

CANDLE UNITY 3

Lighting this candle represents the lighting the life of two people in love. Marriage takes two people working together to keep it aflame.

CANDLE UNITY 4

This candle is also a candle of Unity because you have both come together like moths to a flame. Bring a spark within yourself to create an even brighter light.

CANDLE UNITY 5

As you light this candle today, may the brightness of the flame shine throughout your lives giving you the strength to be supportive and understanding. Giving you reassurance in the darkness and enjoyment in the light.

CANDLE UNITY 6

Will you please take a candle and together ignite the larger one. This flame is a glowing reminder that your lives burn with the intensity of love. Ensure you do your utmost to keep that intensity alight.

CANDLE UNITY 7

Bride and Groom, these individual candles represent your individual families and friends. Lighting the center candle represents that your two lives are now being joined together as one aflame with love. Please pick up the lighted candles and together light the center candle.

CANDLE UNITY 8

Bride and Groom have chosen to affirm their love by the lighting of a unity candle. They have asked their families to participate in this ceremony.

Each of us has an aura of light and when two souls that are destined for each other find one another, their streams of light flow together and their auras glow brighter and stronger, united as one.

CANDLE UNITY 9

Fire is associated with the home and family, as the warmth of the hearth and the "home fires." Today Bride and Groom will each take a candle and light the center candle thereby unifying the light. The flame symbolises the beauty and vitality of a love that will burn eternal.

CANDLE UNITY 10

Bride and Groom will light the outside candles representing the light of their individual selves, families and friends. Then together they will light the unity candle signifying the fusion of their life, family and friends as one flame.

CANDLE UNITY 11

Bride and Groom As you set this candle alight you signify two hearts set aflame burning with love for each other. Once separate, now alight with the warmth of loving hearts.

CANDLE UNITY 12

This candle represents the light of your essence. All that makes you who you are. Fire is one of the basic elements on earth. Once worshipped as the source of life itself. As you merge your flames to light the third candle, you celebrate the power of separate lights to ignite a common flame of passion and commitment that come together as one.

Candle Unity 13

Let the lighting of these candles reflect your thoughts on this day. Your separate pathways lighting your way to the future. Two people destined to find each other. To bring light into each other's life. To shine with the light of hope.

Candle Unity 14

A very beautiful way to symbolise the marriage of Bride and Groom is to invite their mothers to come forward and light the individual candles which represent the two separate families. Today is lit a love spell to call forth enduring romance and passion. The moon was waxing and so we set it alight. It flickered a moment and then burnt bright.

Candle Unity 15

Throughout history, many different societies have used candle lighting to celebrate and acknowledge special holidays and events. Lighting candles honours those we love. Today Bride and Groom will take their individual candles and light the large candle in the center, representing their unity in marriage and the honour with which they will respect it.

Candle Unity 16

Groom and Bride come together today to unify as one. Just as this one light cannot be divided, nor will their lives be divided. They come into their marriage relationship as individuals and they do not lose their identity, rather they use their individuality to create and strengthen the relationship of marriage. The two candles lit signify the coming together of two people from two families and the unity candle symbolises the new family you are now forming from your past lives. The flames will burn brighter when joined together. Now you both are charged with keeping the flame of your marriage bright for the rest of your days.

CANDLE UNITY 17

The two candles that have been placed here will now be lit by members of both families to represent the lives of Bride and Groom to this moment. These burning lights represent the inner light of faith, wisdom and love that Bride and Groom have received from their parents. Bride and Groom will now light the centre candle, representing the union of their lives and families.

CANDLE UNITY 18

Bride and Groom will now light the Unity Candle to symbolise the union of their lives. From now on their thoughts shall be for each other, their joys and sorrows shall be shared alike and they accept the individuality of each other as a means of fulfilling their union as one entity.

CANDLE UNITY 19

Bride and Groom, will now light these individual candles which represent their separate personalities. Groom and Bride you have special qualities, talents, and passions. Appreciate these things and never attempt to extinguish each other's inner radiance.

Please take your separate candles and join them together to light the unity candle of marriage, symbolizing your shared values and commitment. Just as a candle will extinguish itself without air, so shall your marriage if you do not give each other breathing room. Share closeness, yet allow each other room to breathe. Like the flame of this candle, give freely of warmth, comfort, and guidance. On future wedding anniversaries, please light a candle together and renew your promises to each other. As your life unfolds, frequently renew your commitment to each other and remind yourselves often of what brought you together.

CANDLE UNITY 20

The Unity Candle Ceremony symbolises your two lives becoming one with the flame of love that burns at the heart of every family. It invites your parents to light the candles of love and unity, passing this flame on to you, the next generation. It recognizes the importance of family and tradition as you go forth in your new role of husband and wife.

CELTIC RING WARMING

Ladies and Gentleman. Bride and Groom ask that you now participate in an ancient Celtic tradition. The blessing and warming of their wedding rings. The rings will be passed amongst you and I ask that as you hold the rings momentarily, will you please offer a silent wish or blessing to the couple for their married life together and then pass them to the next person. May the seamless circle of these rings become a symbol of Bride and Groom's endless love.

RING WARMING 1

Bride and Groom have chosen to exchange rings as a symbol of their vows. Wedding rings are the most visible sign of the bond two people make. A commitment to life, to each other and to the future. These rings will not only be a gift from one to another but will be given with the love, support and wisdom of their family and friends.

I now ask the Bride and Groom's families to warm these rings by passing them down the row. As you hold them in your hands, pause for a moment and make a silent wish for Bride and Groom's future before you pass them on to the next person.

RING WARMING 2

During this ceremony Bride and Groom will exchange rings. Their rings are a visible sign of their commitment to one another. I now invite family and friends to take part in the warming of the rings. I ask that you wish Bride and Groom health, happiness and all that is noble in life. I ask that each guest as the rings are passed to you hold them for a moment. Warm them with your love and make a silent wish for this couple and their future together.

When these rings come back they will contain, that which is more priceless than gold. Your love, hope and pledge of support for their marriage.

Ring Warming 3

Before Bride and Groom repeat their vows and exchange rings, they have asked that family and friend participate in the "blessing of their rings." The rings will now be passed amongst you. As you hold the rings take the opportunity to silently wish Bride and Groom health, happiness.

Ring Warming 4

Bride and Groom will exchange rings as a symbol of their love and commitment to one another. They ask for your blessings upon their marriage. As the ceremony proceeds they would like to invite family and friends to take part in the warming of their rings. When the rings make their way to you please take a quick moment to hold them, warm them with your love, and silently make a wish or ask a blessing for this couple and their future together. When these rings return they will contain your blessings of love and support for this union to keep it strong throughout the years.

CHILDREN'S CANDLE

Express your love and welcome your children into your new blended family by including them in your candle-lighting ceremony.

If you have children whom you want to honour during the wedding ceremony, use candles to represent yourself the Bride and Groom and candles to represent each child, or if there are numerous children, the one candle representing them all.

Wording

The lighting of the center candle represents not only the union of Bride and Groom in marriage, but also the unity formed in this new family, in which your lives will now shine as one. Or if you are blending two families: "As you light your candles, and the flames become one, let this signify the blending of two families."

Often marriage is viewed as the union of two persons, yet marriages not only unite the Bride and the Groom, they unite families. With the changing structure of what a family is in today's world marriage offers unique and wonderful opportunities to increase the number of loving caring relationships we have in our lives.

During a wedding ceremony rings are exchanged with a promise. Bride and Groom thought appropriate that their children should also receive a token of their promise to them this day. They wanted to find a way to let them know now how special and they are in their own way, and how blessed they feel to love them.

CHILDREN IN THE CEREMONY

Often marriage is viewed as the union of two persons, yet marriages not only unite the Bride and the Groom, they unite families. If either the Bride or Groom already has a child, or children from a former marriage, or of their own, they may include the children in the wedding ceremony. This is usually done after the ring ceremony.

CHILDREN IN THE CEREMONY 1

During a wedding ceremony rings are exchanged with a promise:

Groom and Bride thought it appropriate that their children should also receive a token of their promise this day. The giving of a token signifies how special and wonderful the children are each in their own way and how blessed Bride and Groom feel to be parents.

CHILDREN IN THE CEREMONY 2

Bride and Groom, the rings you have given to one another are not only symbols of your commitment to one another, they are more. Today you are also making a commitment to the children (names). You are pledging your love to them as well. Confirming that you will be supportive as a family together. Let the circles of the wedding ring signify the circle of love and commitment that embraces the children and the two of you as family.

Consider these words from the Prophet:

You may give them your love, but not your thoughts, for they have their own thoughts. You may house their bodies but not their souls, for they dwell in the house of tomorrow, which you cannot visit, not even in your dreams. You may strive to be like them, in their innocence, but seek not to make them like you. For life goes not backward nor tarries with yesterday. You are the bows from which your children as living arrows are set forth.

CHILDREN IN THE CEREMONY 3

As a couple you both have had the responsibility of leading an honourable life raising children and doing your utmost in maintaining a harmonious relationship. Today is a special moment and the vows chosen reflect your love by involving your children (names). Today you both look forward with optimism, to a new era in your life. As a committed couple, you are affirming your children, your devotion and attention, as well as your love.

CHILDREN IN THE CEREMONY 4

In the coming years, with concentration and confidence you can strengthen your love and affection for each other. In doing this, you are also teaching your children values of life and its essence. When you both express loyalty and trust in each other, your children learn life lessons. You are also laying a foundation and leaving a legacy of principles and cherished values.

CHILDREN IN THE CEREMONY 5

The responsibility of raising children and maintaining a relationship is a lifelong exercise of humility, integrity and commitment. Today is a special moment and the vows chosen reflect your love by involving the children (names).

CHRISTIAN CEREMONY

Dearly Beloved, We are gathered here today in the sight of God to celebrate one of life's greatest moments. Marriage is an honorable estate created by God and signifying unto us the mystical union between a man and a woman.

Who is it that brings this woman to this man?

Bride and Groom, only love will maintain a marriage. As you travel through life together remember that the true measure of success, the true avenue to joy and peace, is to be found within the love you hold in your hearts. Hold the key to your heart very tightly.

Personal Vows

Do you promise to love, honour and protect Bride/Groom, forsaking all others and holding only to him/her?

OR

Do you promise to love, honour and protect him/her, forsaking all others and holding only to him/her?

Do you take Bride/Groom to be your wife/husband? To have and to hold, in sickness and in health, for richer or for poorer, and I promise my love to you forevermore.

Corinthians 13

A marriage ceremony represents one of life's greatest commitments, but also is a declaration of love. I will now read to you what Paul wrote of love in a letter to the Corinthians.

Love is patient, love is kind. It does not envy, it does not boast, it is not proud. It is not rude, it is not self-seeking, it is not easily angered, and it keeps no record of wrongs. Love does not delight in evil but rejoices with the truth. It always protects, always trusts, always hopes, and always perseveres. Love never fails.

RINGS

Wedding rings are an outward and visible sign of an inward spiritual grace, signifying to all the uniting of Bride and Groom in marriage.

I give you this ring, as a token and pledge, of my constant faith and abiding love.

PROCLAMATION

Bride and Groom. Today you unite as husband and wife affirming your faith and love for one another. Remember to cherish each other as special and unique individuals and respect the thoughts, ideas and suggestions of one another.

PRONOUNCEMENT AS HUSBAND AND WIFE

Bride and Groom, insomuch as the two of you have agreed to live together in Marriage. Have sealed your love for each other by these vows and the giving of rings I now declare you to be husband and wife. Congratulations, you may kiss your Bride.

COMMITMENT CEREMONY

Hello, and welcome to the celebration of the unique and wonderful union between Bride and Groom. Today, in front of friends and family you honour your commitment to each other. Today you proclaim your love to the world and we rejoice with you.

In presenting yourselves here today you perform a remarkable act of faith. This faith can mature and endure, but only if you both determine to make it so. A lasting and growing love is never automatic, nor guaranteed by marriage. It requires maturity, commitment and inner strength. Let the foundation of your marriage be the love you have for each other.

Faults will appear where now you find contentment, and wonder can be crushed by the routine of daily living. But today you resolve that your love will never be suppressed by the commonplace, obscured by the ordinary, or compromised by life's difficulties.

Stand fast in that hope and confidence, and believe in your shared future just as strongly as you believe in yourselves and in each other today. Only in this spirit can you create a partnership that will sustain all the days of your lives. Bride and Groom, we are here to celebrate as you begin this journey together.

Vows

I promise above all else to live in truth with you and to communicate with you. I give you my hand and my heart as a sanctuary of warmth and peace and pledge my love, devotion, faith and honour as I join my life to yours.

I take you to be my partner for life. I promise to listen and communicate with you. I give you my heart as a sanctuary of comfort and peace. I pledge my love, devotion, and honour as I join my life to yours.

Ring Exchange

Wedding rings are made precious by our wearing of them. They are a symbol of significant importance. Your rings say that you have made the choice to share your life with someone for eternity.

COIN OR ARRAS CEREMONY

This was originally a Roman custom of dividing gold, or silver into equal halves by both parties as a pledge of marriage representing the Groom's dedication to the welfare of the Bride, and signifying the Bride and Groom's hope for wealth, prosperity and security. It eventually became a Spanish custom. Thirteen gold unity coins are presented to the Bride by the Groom, signifying he will support her. The number 13 represented Christ and his 12 apostles.

This ceremony can be done after the Bride and Groom exchange their vows and rings.

The Groom gives the Bride thirteen gold unity coins as a symbol of his unquestionable trust and confidence. The symbolism, which may be explained by the Celebrant, is that the Groom recognises his responsibility as a provider, and pledges his ability to support and care for her. The Bride's acceptance signifies her trust and confidence in her Groom.

The Unity coins are presented to the Celebrant. The Celebrant then blesses the coins and hands them to the Bride who places them in the Groom's cupped hands. The Groom will then pour the unity coins into the Bride's cupped hands. This represents his giving her control of all his worldly goods. They are then placed into a container as a family keepsake.

Now let us do an exchange of the Arras, or coins.

Instruction: (Name) will present the pillow with the coins to the Celebrant.

The coins are a reminder that a couple will mutually support each other, their children and the world around them.

May God/the universe bless these coins that symbolise mutual support and responsibility.

The Celebrant drops the coins into Groom's waiting hands.

The Groom then repeats after Celebrant:

Bride, I give you this coin as a pledge of my dedication to your welfare.

The Groom then drops the coins into his Bride's hands.

The Bride repeats after Celebrant:

I accept them and in the same way pledge my dedication to you, the care of our home, and the welfare of our children.

The Bride then puts her hand above the Groom's and drops the coins back into his hands.

The Groom then hands the coins to his Best Man for safe-keeping.

DOVE RELEASE

The pigeon's ability to return home from long distances has long baffled all scientists. No one quite knows how they find their way home, but they think it is possibly linked to the Sun's position and the Earth's magnetic fields at any given time, although memory and landmarks may also play a role. Once the birds are released, it is their nature to want to return home to their mates and offspring. The birds will circle the area, get their bearings and then head home. This is the reason homing pigeons should be used for releases instead of the much smaller, fragile white ring neck doves.

These birds are capable of returning home from hundreds of kilometres away, but it sometimes takes many hours for them to fly that great a distance. Therefore, it is best to limit them to shorter distances because of the time the releases take place. Please do your homework on this before making a decision as to whether they will be appropriate at your ceremony. You have to allow the birds enough time to return home before dark. That's why they can't be released at night weddings.

Many photo opportunities have been missed due to the doves being released at the wrong time due to the releasers not having the correct hold on the doves. Also there is a greater chance of the bird have a normal body function and soiling on you. To avoid this and injury to the people and the birds it is best to only have cage/basket releases.

The birds cannot be released under the following conditions: thunder, lightning, heavy rain, high winds, extreme heat. Doves do mate for life or until one of the partners dies. This lifelong commitment is one of the reasons doves are a popular symbol for marriage.

WORDING FOR DOVE RELEASE

DOVE RELEASE 1

White doves are the symbol of Love, Peace and Hope. They pair for life, and at the end of each day, they return to the same home for the night.

As Groom and Bride release these doves, we ask you, their family and friends, to witness this very symbolic gesture, which heralds the beginning of their new life together.

Bride and Groom we wish you love. That, like the doves, soars to the heavens. We wish you peace as you work together to develop a home and we join in your hope for a long and happy marriage.

DOVE RELEASE 2

Doves are not by each other's side for every hour of every day. In the evening, however, whether their day's journey has been together or apart, both doves return to the same home for the night, just as a married couple return to each other's loving arms and the comfort of their home at night.

Bride and Groom, as the doves fly they will carry your wishes for peace, love and hope for your future life together.

Dove Release 3

Releasing white doves creates a truly magical effect at a wedding. The white dove has been an emblem of peace, love and harmony for many centuries. As a symbolic gesture Bride and Groom are now going to release two white birds. They will fly into the sky and circle above us a few times to get their bearings before they fly home together. This symbolises our newlywed couple setting off on their journey together as a married couple seeking new beginnings. Bride and Groom may your marriage fly on the wings of peace, harmony and eternal love.

Dove Release 4

Groom and Bride, as you begin your new journey as husband and wife; we release this pair of two white birds. They will fly upwards and circle above us a few times, then fly home together as a pair. This symbolises our newlywed couple setting off on their life together, in harmony, such is the miracle of love.

Dove Release 5

For centuries, the White Dove has been a symbol of Peace, Love and New Beginnings.

As a romantic gesture, Groom and Bride are now going to release these two white doves. They will fly upwards, perhaps circle above us a few times, and then fly home together, as a pair. This symbolises our newlywed couple setting off on their journey in life together, in harmony.

Groom and Bride, we wish for you, that your life together will be long, rich and rewarding. May your marriage carry with it all the wonderful qualities that these birds represent, flying off to find food to feed their families, to find materials to build their nest, to support their family and to come home to rest?

Dove Poem - Author Unknown

Two doves meeting in the sky.
Two loves hand in hand, eye to eye.
Two parts of a loving whole.
Two hearts and a single soul.
Two stars shining big and bright.
Two fires bringing warmth and light.
Two songs played in perfect tune.
Two flowers growing into bloom.
Two Doves gliding in the air.
Two loves free without a care.
Two parts of a loving whole.
Two hearts and a single soul.

POEM – Winged Flight

From today this winged love begins its flight across the skies of time. It will fly above the bounds of earth and beyond the edge of now, for when hearts and minds come together as one, the union takes mere mortals to places never been. The flight of love will allow you to challenge your wildest dreams. Side by side you will explore the endless possibilities of your shared world and your journey will soar and fly with bearings sound and direction true.

May your winds be favourable and your skies remain clear, as you guide your shared flight towards the rising sun, for in the dawn of each new day you will find the light to guide your way.

May you enjoy your journey along the way, and may you feel the gentle guiding presence of others who share the skies with you, the place of freedom, adventure and endless hope.

Entrance of the bride

First to walk down the aisle is the ring bearer although sometimes they stand with the Groomsmen. Then the flower girls. The Bridesmaids (unless they follow after the Bride holding her veil). The Bride makes her entrance on the arm of her father, brother, mother, parents, her older child or children, or she may choose to walk with a sister or even the Groom or person of her choice.

OR

If the Bride chooses to walk alone, somewhere along the way she may be met by the Groom, and escorted by him to where they will stand during the ceremony.

Thou shalt love and be loved by me forever.

A hand like this hand shall throw open the gates of new life to thee!

Robert Browning

Follow the Passion of Your Heart!

FAMILY BLESSINGS

FAMILY BLESSINGS 1

I ask now. Who blesses this marriage of Bride and Groom? Both families respond: We do!

FAMILY BLESSINGS 2

Would the parents/family of Bride and Groom please stand.

I ask you as parents/family, do you promise to support Bride and Groom as a couple in the new relationship into which they are about to enter? Both families respond: We do!

FAMILY BLESSINGS 3

Will the families of Bride and Groom please stand

As Bride and Groom join their lives in marriage, they also bring their families together in a new relationship, creating new bonds of trust and ties of affection. Will you give them your love, your blessings and your support? Both families respond: We Will!

FAMILY BLESSINGS 4

Will everyone please stand

Family and Friends, Bride and Groom have invited you here because you are important people in their lives. Your love and support will be important always. Will all of you do everything in your power to assist this marriage? Will you do your best to give your love, your blessings and your support? Congregation: We will!

Family Blessings 5

Bride or Groom entering into a marriage where there are children

Bride/Groom, you are entering a new family. Will you give to them your trust, understanding and affection? Will you do your utmost to be considerate and loving parents to (children's names)?

Family Blessings 6

Bride and Groom you are entering a union not just with each other, but one that involves (children's names). Do you both promise to do your best in sharing the responsibilities of assisting (children's names) to grow, and enjoy their lives through affection and respect. Bride and Groom: We will!

Family Blessings 7

To Bride and Groom. Bride and Groom you are entering a new family. Will you give to them your trust, love and affection? Will you do your utmost to be faithful and loving parents to (children's names)? Bride and Groom: We will!

FAMILY MEDALLION

The family medallion is a symbol for family unity. It can be presented as a gift on any family occasion to include recognition of the children. The medallion has three circles representing the two families coming together and the child. The Family Medallion ceremony is a way to include children in the wedding ceremony. This is a great way to build a bond between step-parents and step-children. The recognition of children offers an opportunity for your guests to bear witness not only to your vows as husband and wife but your family commitment as well.

Wording

We think of a wedding as the union of two people, when in reality it is much broader. It is a coming together of families.

Parents Pledge

(Child/Children's name/s), we want you to know you are very important in our lives and we promise to love you and care for you. We give you this medallion to wear to show how important you are to us and the special place you have in our lives.

We give thanks, for the relationship we are celebrating today and are humbled by the recognition that today we face a new future. One where love is unfolding and encompassing our families.

FAMILY MEDALLION 1

(Insert Child/rens Names), you will have a share in this marriage, for your lives will be touched by the promises made by your mother and father today.

We now ask you to promise that you will all join together and work to create a family of consideration, respect and support.

We ask that you help to create a home and a way of life in which all of you may grow into the best people you can be. In this spirit, will you pledge to continue to grow together and honour this new family for all the days that follow?

The child/ren respond, " I will/We will".

Bride and Groom, as you give yourselves to one another in love and loyalty, will you also promise always to keep room in your new life together for (Insert child/rens names)? Will you commit yourselves to respect and honour them as individuals and members of this family? Will you pledge to cherish, encourage and tenderly care for them as long as they need you?

Bride and Groom respond, "We will".

As a symbol of the two families joined as one today, a special medallion will now be presented to each of you.

As you receive your token of family unity, always remember the love that has brought all of you together and that will guide you and nurture you in the years ahead.

FAMILY UNITY CANDLE CEREMONY – CHILDREN

An option for blending family weddings is to include the children in the unity candle ceremony. Children, who are old and responsible enough, can participate in the Unity Candle ceremony. Here are a few options:

If only one or two children are involved, they can be given their own tapers and join the Bride and Groom in lighting the pillar candle. However, if more than two children are involved, they should receive their own tapers, but rather than light the pillar candle, light their tapers from it.

The candle lighting ceremony is a perfect opportunity for children who are old enough to congratulate the Bride and Groom and acknowledge the new family union. They can each say, or read something, or do so in unison.

"Light this candle, as a symbol of your life and hopes together and the two families who are joined in your marriage."

FAMILY VOWS BLENDING

Blending family vows, is appropriate, even encouraged when the marriage will create a new family with children. That is, the Bride, the Groom, or both have children. It is important to welcome the children as a part of the new family created by the union. When you compose your vows to them, include an introduction and acknowledgement of the children. A warm welcome to the family. Your commitment as a parent and your pride in having each individual child as part of your now larger family. In fact, right after both the Bride and Groom bestow the children with their vows, is a perfect time to present each child with a special gift such as a piece of jewellery, a ring, pendant or a stuffed toy or book.

FAMILY VOWS 1

We commit ourselves to (*children/s names*), promising to help guide you through life, during good times and bad. We promise to love you, support you and work together as a family.

FAMILY VOWS 2

Together, we promise to love and respect our family. We promise to help you in every step that you take in your life. This is our gift to you to show you how special we think you are.

GIVING AWAY THE BRIDE

The giving away of the Bride is a traditional part of the ceremony that allows the parents of the Bride and the Groom to be part of the wedding ceremony

GIVING AWAY 1

Who gives this woman to be married to this man?

GIVING AWAY 2

Who gives this man and woman to be married to each other?

GIVING AWAY 3

May I ask that the parents of Bride and Groom to please rise.

This wedding is a celebration of family. It is the union not only of Bride and Groom but of two families. In blending the different lifestyles and traditions they thereby strengthen their family tree.

To honour the uniting of the families, I now ask both Bride and (Groom's) parents for their blessing. Do you offer your love, support and goodwill?

Parents Say: We do.

GIVING AWAY 4

I ask those assembled. Do you pledge to honour and support this marriage with love?

GIVING AWAY 5

I now ask those assembled. Families and friends will you embrace this marriage with love and the joy of sharing your lives with Bride and Groom?

"We will."

GIVING FLOWERS TO MOTHERS OF THE BRIDE AND GROOM

You may wish to present your respective mothers, grandmothers, or special persons with flowers at some stage during the ceremony. This can be done as a surprise at some stage in the ceremony. Perhaps after the lighting of the Unity Candle or marriage blessing. The couple moves to the special person/s they wish to recognise and gives that person a hug and kiss and the glower or gift. This is often a good time for background music to be played or a solo song sung or a poem reading.

GIVING FLOWERS CEREMONY 1

The love that you feel for one another is the flowering of a seed your mothers planted in your hearts many years ago.

Their love for you gave you the skills needed to be able to love others. Their love for you has brought them great happiness and did not diminish when it meat challenges as your evolved. That is the important lesson you can bring into your marriage.

As you embrace one another in your love, so too do you embrace the families that have been brought together on this happy occasion. As a token of gratitude for your families, I would like to ask you to offer these flowers to your mothers as symbols of love and gratitude to not only your mothers, but your families.

Giving Flowers Ceremony 2

Bride and Grooms love for one another. Their sharing and kindness towards each other is the result of childhood learning.

Today, they embrace each other in their love and they also embrace their families, who have come together to celebrate with them on this happy occasion.

As a sign of the deep love they have for their families, Bride and Groom would like to offer these beautiful flowers to their mothers as a loving promise that no matter how far they may sometimes travel, they will always have you in their thoughts and hearts.

Giving Flowers Ceremony 3

Marriage brings together not only a couple, but their families as well. All families are unique. They may come from different backgrounds and ideals, beliefs and opinions but a marriage between their children that unifies them in loyalty and support of their children is significant. To show their appreciation Bride and Groom wish to gift these bouquets of flowers to their mothers.

Today we unite these families by the marriage of Bride and Groom. Bride and Groom would like to acknowledge the love and sacrifice that their parents have made to assist their children to where they are today, a man and woman who are ready to be in a committed, loving marriage of their own. To show their appreciation they will now give their mothers a rose.

GIVING FLOWERS CEREMONY 4

The love that Groom and Bride feel for one another is a seed that their parents planted in their hearts years ago and today it has blossomed. As they embrace each other in their love, they also embrace their families, who have come together on this happy occasion. As a sign of their love for their families, Bride and Groom would like to offer these roses, to their mothers as symbols of their heartfelt love.

GIVING FLOWERS CEREMONY 5

A wedding is the blending of two families, separate lives united from this day forward. This wedding is a celebration of family. Bride and Groom wish to honor and thank you for your patience, wisdom, support, and especially your unconditional love that has been so freely given to them throughout their lives,

GIVING FLOWERS CEREMONY 6

Parents plant love and consideration so that their children may successfully harvest a fruitful life. It is the foundation of this love and caring that Bride and Groom would like to acknowledge today. It takes love and sacrifice to rear a child to adulthood and it is a parent's greatest desire that their child find someone who will care for them, respect them and love them all their life. Today Bride and Groom honour their family by giving their mothers a symbolic gift of beauty, the giving of a rose.

Giving Flowers Ceremony 7

Today, as they embrace one another in their love, Bride and Groom also embrace their families in their hearts for without you love and support they would not be here today. As a sign of their love for their families, Bride and Groom would like to offer these corsages, to their mothers, as symbols of family love.

Giving Flowers Ceremony 8

Marriage is a coming together of two lives and a celebration of the love of two people. Bride and Groom would like their families to know that your efforts were not in vain and that your love and support in the past and offered for the future is very much appreciated. They thank you for the positive principles you have instilled in them.

HAND FASTING

The hand fasting ritual dates back to the time of the ancient Celts. A couple were literally bound together to symbolise a couples love and commitment.

The couple stands together with wedding guests forming a circle around them. No clergy was needed. The couple simply pledged themselves and had their hands gently bound together with a cord or strip of cloth or tartan. The expression "tying the knot" may have come from the hand-fasting ceremony. Hand fasting was originally a trial marriage contract that lasted for a year and a day, if it didn't work out the couple went their separate ways.

It can involve using ribbons or cords. Usually the ribbons or cords are approximately 3 metres long and a couple of centimetres wide. One cord can be used or if you wish to have elaborate wording or meaning, more. Anyone can do the binding. The Celebrant, parents of the Bride and Groom, attendants, brothers or sisters of the couple, relatives or friends.

The hands can be bound is a couple of ways. This is a matter of personal choice.

1. Right hands joined in a handshake position.

2. Left hands joined in a handshake position.

3. Four hands joined with wrist on top of each other forming a figure eight.

4. Holding hands out in front position.

If the couple is from different countries, this is a nice time for them to say a reading or vow in their own language to each other.

HANDFASTING 1

Celebrant: Groom and Bride please turn and look into each other's eyes and hold hands. Will you honour and respect one another, and seek to protect that honour?

Groom and Bride: *We Will* (the first cord is draped over the hands)

Celebrant: And so the binding is made. Will you share each other's discomfort and seek to ease it?

Groom and Bride*: We will* (the second cord is draped over the hands)

Celebrant: Will you share the burdens of each other, so that you may grow as a couple?

Groom and Bride: *We will* (the third cord is draped over the hands)

Celebrant: Will you share each other's laughter, and look for the positive in each other?

Groom and Bride: *We will* (the forth cord is draped over the hands)

Celebrant: And so the binding is made.

Groom and Bride: As your hands are bound together now, so your lives and spirits are joined in a union of love and trust. Above you are the stars and below you is the earth.

Like the stars, your love should be a constant source of light, and like the earth, a firm foundation from which to grow.

Note: The cords/ribbons can be 4 different colours to symbolise the 4 seasons, or any virtues/values that you specially wish to make part of your marriage.

A search on colour meanings will assist here.

Handfasting 2

Bride, please hold Groom's hands palms up, so you may see the gift that they are to you.

These are the hands of your best friend, young and strong and vibrant with love that are holding yours on your wedding day, as he promises to love you all the days of his life.

These are the hands that will work alongside yours, as together you build your future, as you laugh and cry, as you share your innermost secrets and dreams. These are that hands that will passionately love you and cherish you through the years, for a lifetime of happiness.

These are the hands that will countless times wipe the tears from your eyes: tears of sorrow and tears of joy. These are the hands that will comfort you in illness, and hold you when fear or grief engulfs your heart.

These are the hands that will tenderly lift your chin and brush your cheek as they raise your face to look into his eyes: eyes that are filled completely with his overwhelming love and desire for you.

Groom, please hold Bride's hands palms up, so you may see the gift that they are to you.

These are the hands of your best friend, smooth, young and carefree, that are holding yours on your wedding day, as she pledges her love and commitment to you all the days of her life.

These are the hands that will massage tension from your neck and back in the evenings after you've both had a long hard day. These are the hands that will hold you tight as you struggle through difficult times.

These are the hands that will comfort you when you are sick, or console you when you are grieving.

These are the hands that will passionately love you and cherish you through the years, for a lifetime of happiness. These are the hands that will give you support as she encourages you to chase down your dreams. Together as a team, everything you wish for can be realised.

HANDFASTING 3

Groom and Bride hold each other's hands

These are the hands of your best friend, young and strong and full of love for you, that are holding yours on your wedding day, as you promise to love each other today, tomorrow, and forever.

These are the hands that will work alongside yours, as together you build your future.

These are the hands that will passionately love you and cherish you through the years, and with the slightest touch, will comfort you like no other.

These are the hands that will hold you when fear or grief fills your mind.

These are the hands that will countless times wipe the tears from your eyes, tears of sorrow, and tears of joy.

These are the hands that will tenderly hold your children.

These are the hands that will help you to hold your family as one.

These are the hands that will give you strength when you need it.

Lastly, these are the hands that even when aged, will still be reaching for yours, still giving you the same unspoken tenderness with just a touch."

HANDFASTING 4

Welcome family and friends! We come today to celebrate one of life's greatest moments. To give recognition to the worth and beauty of love and to cherish the words that will unite Bride and Groom in marriage.

Bride and Groom, in the days ahead of you there will be times of sadness and times of joy. Harmony will be your reward if you follow this advice.

Let your love be stronger than your anger. Learn the wisdom of compromise, for it is better to bend than to break. Look for the best in your partner and ask for help when you need it. Remember that true friendship is the basis for any lasting relationship. Give your partner the same courtesies and kindness you bestow on your friends. Say "I love you" every day.

We pray that your love will be everlasting. That good fortune shines upon you and lights your way, so that you may give each the sustenance and happiness. Nourish your minds with your wisdom. Enrich your hearts with your love. Feed your marriage with kindness and understanding. May you have the courage and inspiration to honour your vows. May you be supported and encouraged in your union and be eternally blessed. Amen.

Vows

Marriage is a commitment. A precious gift. A lifelong dedication and a daily challenge to love one another more fully and more freely.

Do you promise to be a tender, faithful partner? Do you promise to love, honour and comfort in sickness and in health, for richer, for poorer, for better for worse, from this day forward?

Do you promise to be a tender, faithful partner? To love, honour and comfort in sickness and in health, for richer, for poorer, for better or worse, from this day forward?

Rings 1

These rings, a token of your love for one another, serve as a reminder that all in life is a cycle; all comes to pass and passes away, and comes to pass again.

May your lives, through the reminder of these rings, be blessed with continuing renewal of love, strength and solidarity.

Rings 2

The circle without beginning, without end is a symbol of the cycle of life. Of birth, death and rebirth. This shall serve as a physical reminder of your vow, and that all things begin and end and begin again, as the Universe decrees. These rings shall serve to remind you that life goes on, that these moments pass. When you are engulfed in anger or in sadness, look to your hand and know the wheel of life turns forever onward, and it is love that turns the wheel. Let these rings serve as locks, binding you together in love forever.

Rings 3

I take you my heart at the rising of the moon and the
    setting of the stars.

To love through all that may come in our life together. In
    all our lives,

may we be reborn that we may meet and know and
    love again.

UNITY CANDLE

These two candles before you are representative of yourselves as a separate and complete human being. Together, light the third candle in the center but do not extinguish the first two. For in a life partnership, you do not lose yourself. You add something new. A relationship with the capacity to merge into one another without losing sight of yourself as an individual.

May the brightness of these flames shine throughout you lives. May they give you courage and reassurance in the darkness, warmth and safety in the cold and joy in your bodies, minds and spirits. May your union be forever blessed.

BINDING

Bride and Groom, please hold hands. These are the hands of your best friend. They are holding yours on your wedding day as you promise to love each other today, tomorrow and forever.

These are the hands that will work alongside yours as together you build your future.

These are the hands that will passionately love you and cherish you all through the years and with the slightest touch will comfort you like no other.

These are the hands that will hold you when fear or grief overtakes you.

These are the hands that will give you strength when you need it.

May these hands always reach out with love tenderness and respect.

May these hands continue to build a loving relationship that lasts a lifetime.

May this cord hold your hands together in love, rarely in anger.

May the vows you have spoken never grow bitter in word or deed and may you be blessed with health and prosperity. Remember, what one may not provide, the other may. So you are bound, each to the other, unto all of your days.

Heart to thee, soul to thee, body to thee, forever and always. So mote it be.

Closing

To be loved is to know joy and happiness. To love is to know the joy of sharing oneself. It is through the miracle of love that we discover the fullness of life.

May blessings always be with you guiding you now and forever.

May the sun bring you new energy by day and the moon softly restore you by night. May the rain wash your worries and the breeze blow new strength into your being. May you walk gently through the world and know its beauty all the days of your life and may you live those days in peace, love and happiness.

PRONOUNCEMENT

Bride and Groom, in the binding of yourselves you have created a life anew. Step forth into that new life rejoicing at the magic and rarity of true love. With the blessings of all present, it is an honour to pronounce you husband and wife.

You may seal your vows with a kiss!

PRESENTATION

It is my honour to present Mr. and Mrs.

HAND FASTING CEREMONY 5

As this knot is tied, so are your lives now bound. Woven into this cord, imbued into its very fibers, are all the hopes of your friends and family and of yourselves, for your new life together.

With the fashioning of this knot do I tie all the desires, dreams, love, and happiness wished here in this place to your lives for as long as love shall last.

In the joining of hands and the fashion of a knot, so are your lives now bound, one to another. By this cord you are thus bound to your vow. May this knot remain tied for as long as love shall last.

May this cord draw your hands together in love, never to be used in anger. May the vows you have spoken never grow bitter in your mouths.

As any child discovers when they are learning to tie their own shoes, the first move is to cross the ends. As your hands are bound by this cord, so is your partnership held by the symbol of this knot.

May it be granted that what is done before the gods be not undone by man. Two entwined in love, bound by the desire to make the best of whatever life presents you with a united strength.

Hold tight to one another through both good times and bad striving always to do your best for yourself, your relationship and each other.

Handfasting 6

Know now before you go further, that since your lives have crossed in this life you have formed ties between each other. As you seek to enter this state of matrimony you should strive to make real, the ideals which give meaning to both this ceremony and the institution of marriage.

With full awareness, know that within this circle you are not only declaring your intent to be hand fasted before your friends and family, but you speak that intent also to your creative higher powers. The promises made today and the ties that are bound here greatly strengthen your union; they will cross the years and lives of each soul's growth.

In times past it was believed that the human soul shared characteristics with all things divine. It is this belief which assigned virtues to the cardinal directions; East, South, West and North. It is in this tradition that a blessing is offered in support of this ceremony.

Blessed be this union with the gifts of the East. Communication of the heart, mind, and body Fresh beginnings with the rising of each Sun. The knowledge of the growth found in the sharing of silences.

Blessed be this union with the gifts of the South. Warmth of hearth and home. The heat of the heart's passion. The light created by both to lighten the darkest of times.

Blessed be this union with the gifts of the West. The deep commitment of the lakes. The swift excitement of the river. The refreshing cleansing of the rain and the adventurous passion of the sea.

Blessed be this union with the gifts of the North. A firm foundation on which to build. Fertility of the fields to enrich your lives. A stable home to which you can always return.

Each of these blessings from the four cardinal directions emphasises those things which will help you build a happy and successful union. Yet they are only tools. Tools which you must use together in order to create what you seek in this union.

I bid you look into each other's eyes.

Will you share each other's life and seek to ease any problems in it?

Bride and Groom say, "Yes."

First cord is draped across Bride and Groom's hands and so the first binding is made. Join your hands

Will both of you look for the brightness in life and the positive in each other?

Bride and Groom say, "Yes."

Second cord is draped across Bride and Groom's hands and so the second binding is made.

Will you share the burdens of each so that your spirits may grow in this union?

Bride and Groom say, "Yes."

Third cord is draped across Bride and Groom's hands and so the third binding is made.

Will you dream together to create new realities and hopes?

Yes

Fourth cord is draped across Bride and Groom's hands and so the fourth binding is made.

Will you take the heat of anger and use it to temper the strength of this union?

Bride and Groom say, "We Will."

Fifth chord is draped across Bride and Groom's hands and so the fifth binding is made.

Will you seek to never give cause to break your vows ?

Bride and Groom say, "We shall never do so."

Sixth cord is draped across Bride and Groom's hands and so the sixth binding is made.

The knots of this binding are not formed by these chords but instead by your vows. The cords are removed and placed on altar.

HANDFASTING 7

Your lives have crossed in this life you have formed ties between each other. As you seek to enter this state of matrimony you should strive to make real, the ideals which give meaning to both this ceremony and the institution of marriage.

BLESSING OF THE HANDS

These are the hands that will passionately love you and cherish you through the years, for a lifetime of happiness.

These are the hands that will countless times wipe the tears from your eyes. Tears of sorrow and tears of joy.

These are the hands that will comfort you in illness and hold you when fear or grief touch your mind.

These are the hands that will hold you tight as you struggle through difficult times.

These are the hands that will give you support and encourage you to chase your dreams, so that together everything you wish for can be realised.

Prepare the cords

Today we use these cords to symbolise the binding of promises.

The first promise

Bride and Groom, will you be faithful partners and friends for life?

Bride and Groom say: "We will."

First cord is draped across Bride and Groom's hands and so the first binding is made.

The second promise

Bride and Groom, do you promise to love each other without reservation?

Bride and Groom say: "We will."

Second cord is draped across Bride and Groom's hands and so the second binding is made.

The third promise

Bride and Groom, will you stand together with each other in your times of joy and times of sorrow. Sharing the burdens of each so that your spirits may grow in this union?

Bride and Groom say: "We will."

Third cord is draped across Bride and Groom's hands and so the third binding is made.

THE FORTH PROMISE

Bride and Groom will you always to be open and honest with each other for as long as you both shall live?

Bride and Groom say: "We will."

Fourth cord is draped across Bride and Groom's hands and so the fourth binding is made.

THE FIFTH PROMISE

Will both of you stand by one another in sickness and in health, in plenty and in want?

Bride and Groom say, "We will."

Fifth cord is draped across Bride and Groom's hands and so the fifth binding is made.

THE SIXTH PROMISE

Will you dream and work together to create new realities and hopes for this marriage?

Bride and Groom say, "We will."

Sixth cord is draped across Bride and Groom's hands and so the sixth binding is made.

THE SEVENTH PROMISE

Will you both seek to cherish and strengthen your marriage with respect and honour?

Bride and Groom say, "We will."

Seventh cord is draped across Bride and Groom's hands and so the seventh binding is made.

BINDING OF ALL PROMISES

The knots of this binding are not formed by these chords but instead by your vows. You have tied this knot signifying the binding nature of your vows and of this union.

The cords are removed and placed on signing table.

You can use however many cords/ribbons you wish depending on how many promises you wish to make.

HINDU CEREMONY

A Hindu wedding is a means of spiritual growth where a man and woman become soul mates who can direct their energies into the progress of their souls. The traditional Hindu wedding celebration includes a celebration of the seven steps, which correlate to seven wedding vows on the nature of the marriage commitment. The wedding vows may be recited by the couple, although many couples choose to physically or symbolically represent the wedding vows.

In the vows the Groom vows to consult with his wife and always involve her. Holding hands they take the sapta padi... a seven step symbolic journey through life both exchanging the following vows at the same time with each other.

E.g. The first step to earn a living for their family and respect our bounty. The second step to live a healthy life style. The third step to be concerned for our partner's welfare. The fourth step to live together as friends enjoying happiness and friendship throughout our lives. The fifth step to share with each other and friends and family. The sixth step to be kind and considerate to each other. The seventh step to care for our children for whom we will be responsible and love.

OR

With God as our guide we take the first step to nourish each other. The second step to grow together. The third step to protect our wealth. The fourth step to share our sorrows and joys. The fifth step to love and protect our children.

The sixth step to be together forever. The seventh step to remain lasting friends. Two halves to make a perfect whole.

OR

1. First Step
We promise to take care of each other and pray for abundant blessings and prosperity in our life.

2. Second Step
We promise to look after our physical and mental well-being and lead a healthy married life.

3. Third Step
We promise to protect any prosperity acquiring knowledge, happiness, and harmony by mutual love and trust.

4. Fourth Step
We pledge to live together as friends sharing fortune and understanding through any misfortune in our lives.

5. Fifth Step
We promise to love and care for family, friends and children that share our lives.

6. Sixth Step
We promise to be kind and considerate to each other.

7. Seventh Step
We desire to be together always.

OR

Finally, let us take the seventh step and become true companions and remain lifelong partners by this wedlock.

Two halves to make a perfect whole.

OR

With God/the Universe as our guide, let us take:

The first step to nourish each other

The second step to grow together in wellbeing

The third step to preserve our prosperity

The fourth step to share our joys and sorrows

The fifth step to care for our children

The sixth step to be together forever

The seventh step to remain lifelong friends

After the seventh step Groom says

We are two halves that make a perfect whole

(The wording can be changed to suit individual taste)

JUMPING THE BROOM

African slaves were forbidden to marry in America. They would make a public declaration of their love and commitment by jumping over a broom to the beat of drums. Today, this ritual's significance is used as a symbol for the start of the couple making a home together. It has become popular for African-American couples to "Jump the Broom" at the conclusion of their wedding ceremony. The broom is beautifully decorated and can be displayed in the couple's home after the wedding.

Jumping the broom led to a ritual where sticks were placed on the ground, to jump over representing the couple's new home. The broom was chosen because it has been the household symbol of home throughout history.

Jumping the Broom Ceremony 1

We end this ceremony with the African American tradition of jumping of the broom. Slaves in America were not permitted to marry, so they jumped a broom as a way of ceremonially uniting. Today Bride and Groom will jump this broom to represent leaving behind their single life and moving forward into their life in marriage. If we can have the broom. Bride and Groom please hold hands and get ready to jump together. Now I am going to ask everyone to count with them and at the end of the count of 3 Bride and Groom will jump. Ready everyone. Ready Bride and Groom. Everyone count 1, 2, 3 Jump!

JUMPING THE BROOM CEREMONY 2

Love recognises no barriers. It jumps obstacles. Today Bride and Groom leave behind the past and jump into the future together secure in their love. By taking the leap, they make a gesture of dedication to working together through the tough times ahead, as well as the easy times.

JUMPING THE BROOM CEREMONY 3

Will Smith in the Movie "Hitch" said, "Any man has the chance to sweep any woman off her feet. He just needs the right broom". Well here it is. You have to find something that you love enough to be able to take risks, to jump over the hurdles. Bride and Groom have found indelible love. They are ready to face the future with the courage of their love.

JUMPING THE BROOM CEREMONY 4

Marriage is a leap of faith. It is jumping into the unknown with the greatest confidence that you have found a person of integrity, friendship and love.to build your future with and stand by you through whatever the future may hold. Bride and Groom, by leaving behind your single self and taking a leap of faith into something new, you find out who you are truly capable of becoming.

JUMPING THE BROOM CEREMONY 5

Bride and Groom, in life there will be times when you need to pick up a broom and do some conscious house cleaning.

JUMPING THE BROOM CEREMONY 6

Bride and Groom have chosen to conclude their ceremony today with the tradition of jumping the broom. This tradition symbolizes the transition from being single to that of a married couple. . We place a broom for jumping, which symbolises the entrance of the couple into a new life together. (Broom is laid in front of couple) Sharing a life with another person requires a leap of faith. By taking the leap, Bride and Groom make a gesture of dedication to working together through the ups and downs of life. They leave behind the past and jump into the future together secure in their faith in each other and their love. I ask everyone to please count to three with me and as we do so, shout with joy as they perform their first act of working together as husband and wife. Ready 1, 2, 3, jump! Ladies and gentlemen it is my privilege to present Mr. and Mrs.

JUMPING THE BROOM CEREMONY 7

Bride and Groom chose to conclude todays service with the jumping the broom ceremony. As they jump over this broom, they physically and spiritually cross the threshold into marriage marking the beginning of their life as a married couple. .Jumping the Broom symbolises the sweeping away of the old and the welcoming of the new. Bride and Groom will begin anew with a clean sweep! (Broom is laid in front of couple) Everyone please count with me 1, 2, 3… Jump! (Couple jumps) Ladies and gentlemen it is my privilege to present Mr. and Mrs.

KNOT TYING CEREMONY

A knot-tying ceremony is similar to the unity ceremony but involves a fisherman's knot. The couple ties the knot together to form a very strong knot; the knot only gets tighter with pressure and cannot come undone which represents the couple's strength. Perfect for a nautical wedding!

Knot Tying Ceremony 1

Bride and Groom will be tying a lovers knot. As you intertwine these ribbons, you are symbolising your two lives with their various threads being united as one.

Colours can be varied. The choice is yours.

This white ribbon representing the Bride

The white ribbon represents purity of thought in this loving union. Kindness, consideration, honour and respect.

Purple Strand representing the Groom

The majesty of love is represented in purple. As the husband loves his wife. Working alongside her, respecting her and appreciating her.

Gold Strand representing God/the universe

The divinity of life is represented in Gold. This relationship is initiated by God/ the universe and will be blessed.

The three ribbons or Cord of three strands symbolises the joining of one man, one woman, and God or a child (more ribbons if more than one child) into a marriage relationship.

May we please have the cords? Thank you.

Let this love knot be a reminder of the strength of your love and the binding together of your two hearts. The completed knot is strong representing the inner strength you will need to ensure your marriage is a success through the inevitable changes life brings.

Lasso (lazo cord) ceremony

The Lasso is associated with a wedding prayer during the ceremony. The symbolism of the lasso is to show the union and protection of marriage and the couples promise to always be together side-by-side. As part of the ceremony to symbolise unity, a large loop of white (or whichever colour you choose) ribbon is placed around the necks of the Bride and Groom and draped onto their shoulders. Special members of the wedding party, or the Celebrant, drape the ribbon around the neck and shoulders of the Bride and Groom. Following a blessing, the ribbon is removed from the shoulders of the couple and given to the Bride as a memento of her becoming the lady of the Groom's heart and home.

This cord symbolizes an infinite bond of love you share that keeps your relationship strong in the face of adversity, as well as that you both are no longer two, but one in marriage.

May this cord remind you to face your life together courageously and to be mutual in support of each other in carrying out your duties and responsibilities as a couple.

May your love grow stronger and bind you closer together through the years.

LOVE LETTER CEREMONY

A love letter exchange is a romantic ceremony that will serve as a lasting reminder of the commitments made to one another. Heartfelt letters, encapsulating your thoughts and feelings are locked away in a wine box to be revealed several years into your marriage.

The Love Letter Ceremony gracefully combines the couples affection and love for each other.

The idea:

Bride and Groom write a letter to each other talking about the following:

1. How you felt when you met.

2. How much you have grown from then to now.

3. What you see in each other

4. Your wishes for your future together.

Love Letter Ceremony 1

Bride and Groom have chosen as a couple to perform a Love Letter & Wine Box ceremony. Love can be expressed in a myriad of different methods, but the most timeless and most treasured will always remain the classic love letter

This box contains a love letter from each to the other describing the good qualities they find in one another and the reasons they fell in love.

The letters are sealed in individual envelopes and they have not seen what the other has written.

On the first anniversary this box shall be opened to share and enjoy the letters. A new letter is to then be written and included with the first letter in the box. These two letters will be read on the second anniversary and so on.

Love Letter and Wine Box Ceremony 2

Bride and Groom have chosen as a couple to perform a Love Letter & Wine Box ceremony.

This box contains a bottle of wine, two glasses, and a love letter from each to the other.

The letters describe the good qualities they find in one another, the reasons they fell in love, and their reasons for choosing to marry.

The letters are sealed in individual envelopes and they have not seen what the other has written.

You have created your very own "romantic" time capsule to be opened on your 5th wedding anniversary.

I recommend that you keep the box in a place of honour prominently displayed in your home as a constant reminder of your commitment to each other.

Bride and Groom should you ever find your marriage enduring hardships, you are to as a couple, open this box, sit and drink the wine together, then separate and read the letters you wrote to one another when you were united as a couple in marriage.

By reading these love letters you will reflect upon the reasons you fell in love and chose to marry each other here today. The hope is, however, that you will never have a reason to open this box. If this is the case, you are to open this box to share and enjoy on your 5th year wedding anniversary!

Bride and Groom, you may now seal the box.

Love Letter and Wine Ceremony 3

Like good wine, a great love will deepen and mature with age.

As a part of today's ceremony, Bride and Groom have captured their thoughts leading up to this day in personal notes to each other.

They have asked their parents (or best man / maid of honour or other loved ones) to compose notes as well, containing their thoughts and their most important pieces of advice to the couple for their journey through life together.

These notes will now be sealed in this box to be opened and shared together with a bottle of wine on future anniversary celebrations.

It is at this time I would ask the parents to come forward and place their note and a bottle of wine inside this box. I now ask that Bride and Groom place their notes to each other with a bottle of wine they have selected to share on their anniversaries.

On that joyous day they will get to reflect on the events and emotions they shared on this wonderful day. They can also reminisce about all of the wonderful memories they will have made over the years and dream of all of those yet to come.

I will now seal the box.

LOVE LETTER CEREMONY 4

Bride and Groom would like you to witness a tradition they chose as important to them. They have written love letters to each other. In these letters they have detailed why they fell in love and what they truly admire about the other person.

The letters were sealed before they each could read what the other wrote. The letters will be placed in this box and the box closed to be reopened on the first anniversary.

If ever they find their marriage has hit a rough spot, they will bring out the box, open it and read the letters to remind them of the love that brought them together and the promises they made to each other here today. It is their hope and belief that they will not need the box except in celebration of an anniversary. Each anniversary they will add another note and perhaps a lovely card or small gift as a surprise for the next year.

Bride and Groom, you may now seal the box and I will then read a poem

If I could have just one wish, I would wish to wake up everyday to the sound of your breath on my neck, the warmth of your lips on my cheek, the touch of your fingers on my skin, and the feel of your heart beating with mine... Knowing that I could never find that feeling with anyone other than you.

MARRIAGE BELL

Ringing of bells at weddings is a long tradition that can be traced all the way back to the Celtic lands, where church bells were believed to have the power to ward off evil spirits and grant wishes. Because of that, Celtic newlyweds were blessed with loud ringing of church bells before the wedding which would announce to anyone their newfound happiness. In Scotland, wedding bells were rung at the conclusion of the wedding, just as the married couple was exiting the church. Tradition of ringing bells before and after the wedding successful spread all across the world, becoming one of the most famous parts in the modern church wedding.

Incorporate the ringing of the marriage bell in your wedding ceremony. The bell was usually made of brass and combined the meaning of the Claddagh (love, loyalty and friendship).

The Celebrant can ring a bell as the Bride or Bride and Groom comes down the aisle or child attendants etc. Small bells can be purchased inexpensively. Everyone can ring a bell if you like at the beginning or end of the ceremony. Put your imagination to work. Be creative with the wording. Ring in the love!

RINGING BELLS CEREMONY 1

(Ringing bell) Bride and Groom hear the toll of this bell. From this day forward let a bell forever remind you of the promises you have made today. Your vows bind you in thought word and deed from this moment forward to the end of your days. If you are faithful in these promises your love and devotion will be fulfilled.

Ringing Bells Ceremony 2

We ring in blessings this day for Bride and Groom. We ring to ward off negative spirits and encourage good. We ring out the old and ring in the new. We ring this bell Bride and Groom as a sign of love and to wish you well. We ring in laughter. We ring in joy. We ring this bell for your wedded bliss. We ring for your love to last forever. May the tinkling sound always convey the love and good wishes hoped for you this day!

MEMORY CANDLE

You may choose to commemorate the memory of deceased relatives or friends, by lighting a candle for them. Usually this will be done before the wedding ceremony begins. The Celebrant explains the tribute, e.g. this memorial candle is being lit in memory of (name and relationship) a photograph of the person/persons can also be placed on the signing table with a small card saying "In memory of (name and relationship)". Then either the Bride or Groom, or the two together, will light the memory candle or candles.

Memory Wording 1

Bride and Groom would like to thank each one of you for sharing this happiest of days with them. They would also like to acknowledge those who are here in spirit today, (names of deceased) whose love and support will be felt by Bride and Groom always.

Memory Wording 2

Today's ceremony Bride and Groom feel is shared by (name and relationship) who have passed beyond this life. Their role/s in the life/lives of Bride and Groom is/are gratefully remembered and honoured as we share this joyful event. In their memory, let us be silent together for a moment in respect for (name/s of deceased) (moment of silence) Thank you.

Memory Wording 3

Before we begin the ceremony today, Bride and Groom would like us to take a moment of silence to remember those family members today solely in spirit, especially (name and relationship). Bride/Groom appreciates all of the love and support (name) has given her/him/them throughout the years and would like to take a moment to remember him/her today. There is then a short pause.

Memory Wording 4

It is important to Bride and Groom that each of you have been important in their lives, and they look forward to your love and support in the future as they begin life as husband and wife. They also wish to pay tribute to family members and friends who are no longer with us physically, but whose gifts of love and compassion over the years will always be cherished and remembered. We are certain they are here today in spirit. In their memory, let us be silent together for a moment (moment of silence) Thank you.

OATHING STONE

A physical object, such as a stone or piece of wood, was used to help transfer the wedding oaths to the spirit energies present in a sacred location. It served as a kind of mediator between the couple, their ancestors and the sacred site.

Different traditions have been slowly coming back into favour. Ancestors and spirits are commonly acknowledged and respected as empowering. Objects are chosen as good luck charms for luck, or prosperity.

After the ceremony is complete, the newly married company release the stone back to the elements by whatever means is felt as being the most appropriate. It can be tossed into a lake, thrown into the sea, laid reverentially upon a large rock, in a hollow log or placed in your garden bed or home.

Wedding guests can also be given small stones to cast while making a wish for the couple's future happiness. I have also used shells found by the seaside to be cast back whence they came after being bestowed with blessings.

Choose or write wording to suit your designs.

BLESSING

With the blessings of our ancestors we call upon the universe to provide and protect. May our neighbours respect us, trouble neglect us, angels protect us and heaven accept us. May we always have walls for the wind. A roof for the rain. Tea beside the fire. Laughter to cheer us. Those we love near us and all our hearts desire. May our pockets be heavy and our hearts be light, May good luck pursue us each morning and night.

Anon

Pure is the water that replenishes nature giving it new life. A new beginning as these two lives become one. One new life. One new beginning.

Love's Philosophy by Percy Shelley

The fountains mingle with the river and the rivers with
    the ocean.
The winds of heaven mix forever with a sweet emotion.
Nothing in the world is single. All things by a law divine
in one another's being mingle, why not I with thine?
See! The mountains kiss high heaven and the waves clasp
    one another.
Now sister flower would be forgiven if it disdained its
    brother;
and the sunlight clasps the earth and the moonbeams kiss
    the sea.
What are all these kissing's worth, if thou kiss not me?

Beach Wedding by Sheryle Pettifer

As we stand beside the ocean tide, may our love
    always be as
constant and unchanging as these never-ending waves
    that pour
beneath our feet, flowing endlessly from the depths of
    the sea;
Your love came softly upon my heart, just as the
    foam comes

softly upon the sand, and just as there will never be a
 morning
without the ocean's flow, so there will never be a day
without my love for you. I pledge myself to you this day.
Our love will be as unchanging and dependable as
 the tide.
As these waters nourish the earth and sustain life, may my
 constant
devotion nourish and sustain you until the end of time.

ROSE CEREMONY

The Rose Ceremony is simple, yet profoundly moving. The Bride and Groom exchange two roses, symbolizing the giving and receiving of their love for each other throughout their entire married life. In the past, the rose was considered a symbol of love and a single rose always meant only one thing. It means the words "I love you". It is appropriate as a gift from husband to wife.

There are two main ways in which roses can be used. In one, the mothers are given roses as tokens of the Bride and Groom's love for the family. This is often kept a secret from the family until the roses are presented. In the other the Bride and Groom exchange roses.

A Rose/Flower ceremony is a romantic way for the Bride and Groom to exchange their first gifts as husband and wife.

Rose Ceremony 1

Marriage is a coming together of two lives and a celebration of the love of two people, yet it is more. The love that you feel for one another is the flowering of a seed your mothers planted in your hearts many years ago. When you were first born, you were a bundle of diapers and tears and your mothers lost sleep caring for you. Their love for you has brought them great happiness and great challenges and their love did not diminish as they met these challenges. That is the great lesson you can bring into marriage.

As you embrace one another in your love, so too do you embrace the families which have been brought together on this happy occasion. As a token of your gratitude for your families, I would like to ask you to offer these roses, symbols of eternal love, to your mothers. (Both the Bride and Groom can hand the roses to each mother together, offering the mothers kisses if they wish).

ROSE CEREMONY 2

It is important that your service reflects your tastes. You can be as involved as little, or as much as you like in choosing your ceremony wording. There are books in the library and also ideas on the internet which contain ideas to help you in choosing the service wording, e.g. poems, vows, readings. Perhaps you would like to write your own vows, or include something you have seen or heard that reflects your feelings.

Maybe you would like to include, family, friends or children in the service, or some family or cultural influence. Do you want a lengthy service, or a personal shorter one? How romantic would you like the readings to be?

You may wish to include your story in the service, as to how you met, what interests you share, and any difficulties you have overcome to be together. Why you have chosen to marry. The significance of the wedding venue. The qualities you admire in each other and your hopes for the future.

When you meet the Celebrant for the first time, they have information you can look through to get an idea of the style of service you wish. They then write a service for your perusal and feedback on any alteration, deletion or additional content required.

Rose/Flower Ceremony 3

Your gift to each other for your wedding today has been your wedding rings which shall always be an outward demonstration of your vows of love and respect. A public showing of your commitment to each other.

You now have what remains the most honourable title which may exist between a man and a woman. The title of "husband" and "wife."

In the past, the rose was considered a symbol of love and a single rose always meant only one thing. It meant the words "I love you." Therefore it is appropriate that for your first gift as husband and wife that gift would be a single rose.

Please exchange your first gift as husband and wife. (couple exchanges roses)

In some ways it seems like you have not done anything at all. Just a moment ago you were holding one small rose and now you are holding one small rose. In some ways, a marriage ceremony is like this. In some ways, tomorrow is going to seem no different than yesterday, but in fact today, just now, you both have given and received one of the most valuable and precious gifts of life. One I hope you always remember. The gift of true and abiding love within the devotion of marriage.

Bride and Groom, I would ask that where ever you make your home in the future, whether it be a large and elegant home or a small and graceful one, that you both pick one very special location for roses. On each anniversary of this truly wonderful occasion you both may take a rose to that spot as a reminder of the love that brought you together and a recommitment to your vows.

In every marriage there are times where it is difficult to find the right words. It is easiest to hurt those who we most love. It is easiest to be hurt by those who we most love. It might be difficult sometimes to be able to express the words "I am sorry" or "I forgive you" or "I need you" or "I am hurting".

If this should happen, if you simply cannot find these words, leave a rose at that spot which both of you have selected, for that rose then says what matters most of all and should overpower all other things and all other words. That rose says the words: "I still love you." The other should accept this rose for the words which cannot be found, and remember the love and hope that you both share today.

Bride and Groom, if there is anything you remember of this marriage ceremony, it is that it was love that brought you here today, it is only love which can make it a glorious union, and it is by love which your marriage shall endure.

ROSE/FLOWER CEREMONY 4

Groom (handing Bride a long-stemmed white rose). Accept this rose as a symbol of my love. Like our love, it has blossomed from a tiny bud to a breathtaking thing of beauty.

Bride (placing the rose into a vase filled with water): I accept this rose, symbolic of your love, placing it into water, a symbol of life.

Without water, this rose will wither and die.

Groom: Once a year I will give you another beautiful white rose, to affirm our love and the vows spoken here today.

Bride: And once a year I will refill this vase with water, to receive the symbol of our love, and to affirm the vows spoken here today.

Rose/Flower Ceremony 5

There are two kinds of family. The family you are born into and the family you choose through friendship and special relationship. Bride and Groom are blessed with both these families.

This ceremony seeks to honour the continuity as well as the growth and possibilities of these relationships.

In honour of the love Bride and Groom feel towards the loving people in their lives, they invite some of these special people to place a flower in this vase to create a garden of love for us all. As each of them places their flower in a single vase, it will create a new and fuller garden.

Each flower represents an individual, the floral arrangement the interrelationship of these family members and friends. May your relationships continue to grow and bloom.

Rose/Flower Ceremony 6

Bride and Groom, today you have exchanged your gifts of wedding rings. An outward expression of your undying love and a public showing of your commitment to each other. You are also going to receive another gift from each other.

Rose Ceremony

Roses have always been a symbol of love, and a single red rose always says, "I love you."

It is appropriate that your next gift to each other on your wedding day, be a single red rose. In some ways it seems that you have not done anything at all. A moment ago you held one small rose, and now you are holding another. A marriage ceremony is like this. In some ways tomorrow is going to seem no different than yesterday.

But in fact, just now, you have both given and received one of the most valuable and precious gifts of life. One I hope you always remember. You have exchanged the gift of true and abiding love within the devotion of marriage.

Bride and Groom, I would ask that wherever you make your home in the future, whether it be a large and grand home or a small and graceful one, that you both pick one very special location for roses.

In every marriage there are times where it is difficult to find the right words to say what's in your heart.

It might be hard sometimes to say "I'm sorry", "I forgive you"; "I need you" or "I am hurting." If this should happen and you just cannot find these words, leave your spouse a rose in that special spot.

That rose says the words; "I still love you."

The other can accept this rose for the words that cannot be found, and remember that it was love that brought you here today, it is only love which can make it a glorious union, and it is by love which your marriage shall endure.

Rose/Flower Ceremony 7

It is now my privilege to be the first to address you as husband and wife. In the language of flowers, a red rose is the symbol of love.

Will you please exchange your roses? In this exchange, you have given to each other your first gift as husband and wife.

It is our hope that where you make your home, there will be a specially appointed place in it for red roses.

On each anniversary you can celebrate by each of you bringing a rose to the appointed place. Understanding that this rose is an affirmation of your love and an acknowledgement of the vows you have made.

In every marriage it is occasionally difficult to find words to resolve certain issues which may arise. If and when such issues might come to your marriage, if either of you will remember and bring to the appointed place a red rose, the other will see it and understand it as a statement of love and accept it, because love is the gateway to all answers.

Corinthians: "Love is patient, love is kind and envies no one.

Love is never boastful, nor conceited, nor rude; never selfish, and not quick to take offense. Love keeps no score of wrongs; it does not gloat over the other's mistakes, but delights in the truth. There is nothing love cannot face; there is no limit to its faith, hope and its endurance. In a word, there are three great things that last forever:

Faith, hope and love and the greatest of these is love."

ROSE/FLOWER CEREMONY 8

In the elegant language of flowers red roses are a symbol of love, the giving of a single red rose is a clear and unmistakable way of saying the words, "I love you."

For this reason it is fitting that the first gift you exchange as husband and wife would be the gift of a single red rose.

Please exchange your first gift as husband and wife.

You both have given and received one of the most valuable and precious gifts of life. One we hope you always remember. The gift of true and abiding love within the devotion of marriage. Bride and Groom, I would ask that wherever you may make your home, that you choose a special location and at those times when words fail, that you leave a red rose at that spot you have both selected . A rose that will say what matters more than all other words. "I still love you". The other should accept this rose for the words that cannot be found, and remember the love and hope that you both have shared today.

MEDIEVAL CEREMONY

We are gathered here in the sight of God/Creation and his bounty of Angels to join together Bride and Groom in a binding of life. It is an honourable estate, into which estate these two persons present come now to be bound.

At this day of binding, if any man do alleged and declare any impediment, why they may not be coupled together in Matrimony, by God's Law or the Laws of the Realm, then may he speak now or forever hold his peace.

Crowd: Let them marry!

Groom wilt thou have this Woman to be thy wedded wife? Will you now plight your troth to live together after God's/Creations ordinance in the holy estate of Matrimony? Wilt thou love her, comfort her, honour, and keep her, in sickness and in health, and forsaking all other keep thee only unto her, so long as ye both shall live?

Groom: I will.

Bride, wilt thou have this man to be thy wedded husband? Will you now plight your troth to live together after God's/Creations ordinance in the holy estate of Matrimony? Wilt though love, honour and keep him in sickness and in health and forsaking all others, keep thee only unto him so long as ye both shall live?

Bride: I will.

RIBBON CEREMONY

This ribbon close entwines two hearts in love together. Friendships dearest pledge is made in joy forever. United you shall walk through life sharing life's pain and pleasure. Hand in hand you shall strive for achievement in life together. Should the path be rough and thorny, let love sustain and guide you. Should the way be strewn with roses let the joys of life embrace you.

Cord Colour

Dark blue. Safe journey and longevity

Light blue Understanding

Pink Romance, partnership and happiness

Green Health. prosperity luck, fertility and beauty

Red Courage, strength and passion

Yellow Wisdom, harmony healing, home

Silver Creativity and protection

White Peace sincerity and devotion

RING WARMING CEREMONY

Before you say your vows and exchange your rings, the wedding Celebrant will ask everyone, including your wedding party to participate in a ring warming. The ring warming is an opportunity to send the Bride and Groom good luck and love through a silent wish to the rings when passed to them.

Ring Warming 1

Having this love in their hearts for each other Bride and Groom have chosen to exchange rings as a symbol of their vows.

The wedding rings are the most visible sign of the bond these two people are about to make.

A commitment to life, to each other and to the future.

What I now ask Bride and Groom's families to do is to warm these rings by passing them down the row.

As you hold them in your hands, pause for a moment, and make your wishes for the couple and for their future before you pass them on to the next person.

These rings will not only be a gift from one to another but will be given with the love, support and wisdom of their family and friends.

RING WARMING 2

Before Bride and Groom say their vows and exchange rings, they have asked that family and friends participate in the "warming of their rings."

This is a blessing on the rings ceremony. Take the opportunity to wish them health, happiness, and all that is noble and good in life when the rings pass to your care.

Hold them for but a moment and warm them with your love, making a silent wish for the future this couple will share.

When returned, these rings will contain in their precious metals that which is all the more precious, your love and pledge of support for this union.

RING WARMING 3

During this ceremony Bride and Groom will exchange rings. These rings are visible signs of their commitment to one another.

As this ceremony proceeds, we invite family and friends to take part in the warming of the rings. We ask that you wish them health and happiness and all that is noble in life.

We ask that each guest hold the rings for a moment, warm them with your love by making a silent wish for this couple and their future together.

The rings will then contain, in their precious metal, that which is more precious. That which is priceless, your love, hope and pledge of support for their union.

RING WARMING 4

Bride and Groom ask family and friends to support them as they begin their journey today. They also ask for your blessing upon their marriage.

Later in the ceremony Bride and Groom will exchange rings as a symbol of their love and commitment to one another.

As the ceremony proceeds they would like to invite family and friends to take part in The Warming of the Rings.

As the rings make their way through the group please take a quick moment to hold them, warm them with your love, and silently make a wish or ask a blessing for this couple and their future together. When these rings return they will contain your love and support for their union to keep it strong throughout the years.

ROSE CEREMONY

The Rose Ceremony is simple, yet profoundly moving. The Bride and Groom exchange two red roses, symbolizing the giving and receiving of their love for each other throughout their entire married life. In the past, the rose was considered a symbol of love and a single rose always meant only one thing. It means the words "I love you". It is appropriate as a gift from husband to wife.

There are two main ways in which roses can be used. In one, the mothers are given roses as tokens of the Bride and Groom's love for the family. This is often kept a secret from the family until the roses are presented. In the other the Bride and Groom exchange roses.

Rose Ceremony 1

Marriage is a coming together of two lives and a celebration of the love of two people, yet it is more. Your parents love for you has brought them great happiness and great challenges. Their love has not diminished as they met these challenges. That is an important lesson you can bring into marriage.

As you embrace one another in your love, so too do you embrace the families which have been brought together on this happy occasion. As a token of your gratitude for your families, I would like to ask you to offer these roses, symbols of eternal love, to your mothers. (Both the Bride and Groom can hand the roses to each mother together, offering the mothers kisses if they wish).

Rose Ceremony 2

Bride and Groom, you will remember this day for the rest of your lives. Those of us who are already married know that marriage like life brings with it many joys and also many challenges. We also know that love, while beautiful is not always easy. There are days when we may find it hard to express the depth of our love for one another. It is my hope and prayer that the two of you will set aside a special place in your home for roses, ancient symbols of love.

When words fail you, or when the challenges of life or marriage begin to weigh on you, go out and get a rose and put it in that special place in your home, so that your partner will be reminded of this moment and of the love you feel for one another. As a token of that love, I ask you to make these roses gifts of love to one another as a married couple.

In another, roses are exchanged as the Bride and Groom's gifts to one another as a married couple. The Rose Ceremony is usually placed at the end of the ceremony just before being pronounced husband and wife.

Your gift to each other for your wedding today has been your wedding rings, which shall always be an outward demonstration of your vows of love and respect, and a public showing of your commitment to each other. You now have what is the most honourable title, which may exist between a man and a woman. The title of "husband" and "wife." Your first gift as husband and wife was your rings. The second gift you have chosen to give today will be a single rose, for the rose is considered a symbol of love. In marriage tomorrow is sometimes going to seem no different than yesterday, sometimes smooth, sometimes trying. It is during the trying times that the gift of a rose will remind you of the importance of your love for each other.

Rose Ceremony 3

Groom (as he hands his Bride a long stemmed white rose): Bride take this rose as a symbol of my love. It began as a tiny bud and blossomed, just as my love has grown and blossomed for you.

Bride (as she places the rose into a bud vase filled with water): "I take this rose, a symbol of your love, and I place it into water, a symbol of life. For, just as this rose cannot survive without water, I cannot survive without you."

Groom: In remembrance of this day, I will give you a white rose each year on our anniversary, as a reaffirmation of my love and the vows spoken here today.

Bride: I will refill this vase with water each year, ready to receive your gift, in reaffirmation of the new life you have given me and the vows spoken here today.

Groom (as he and his Bride join hands around the rose-filled vase): And so, this rose will be a symbolic memory of my commitment to you this hour, I vow to be a faithful husband to you, to comfort you, honour you, respect you and cherish you for as long as we live.

Bride: (as they continue to hold the vase together): And I commit myself to you, to be a faithful wife, to comfort you, honour you, respect you and cherish you for as long as we live.

ROSE CEREMONY 4

Mark Twain said, "A marriage makes two fractional lives a whole. It gives to two questioning natures a renewed reason for living. It brings a new gladness to the sunshine, and a new fragrance to the flowers, and new beauty to the earth, a new mystery to life."

Bride and Groom please take a handful of petals and toss them outward, in so doing you symbolise your declaration to embrace the world as partners.

[Groom and Bride take petals from a bowl]

Enjoy not only the perfume of one another, but the sweetness of nature and humanity.

With the tossing of the rose petals you have demonstrated your love and respect for nature and your renewal from its source. In your marriage use reason and common sense as your guide. When emotion and intellect combine they provide the foundation of a profound love.

WORDS OF THE ROSE CEREMONY

Your first gift as husband and wife will be a single rose. In the past, the rose was considered a symbol of love and the gift of a single rose meant the word, "I love you." It is therefore appropriate that your first gift as husband and wife will be a single rose.

Please exchange your first gift as husband and wife by exchanging roses.

In some ways it may seem like you have not done much at all. Just a moment ago you were holding one small rose and now you are holding one small rose. In some ways marriage is like this. Tomorrow is going to seem no different than yesterday, but today is different for today you have received one of the most valuable and precious gifts of life than can be bestowed upon another. One I hope you will always remember. The gift of true and abiding love given within the devotion of marriage.

In every marriage there are times when it is difficult to find the right words. It is easy to hurt the one we most love and it may be difficult sometimes to say the words, "I am sorry", "I forgive you", "I need you", or "I am hurting". If this should happen. If you simply cannot find these words, leave a rose at that spot which both of you have selected, for the rose will represent the words, "I still love you". The other should accept this rose for the love with which it is presented and take a moment to remember the love and hope that you both shared here today and the vows you made for eternity.

SAME SEX CEREMONY

When two people are in love and want to create a life together the most natural process for them is to share their happiness with those closest to them. Love is an innate part of who we are, it is our inherent nature and to many our one true purpose in life; is to love each other. Love is found in all places and amongst all people. There are no limits for love and the capacity to love is endless.

A wedding ceremony is the outward form and the highest expression of this love. It celebrates all that love holds for a couple and the brilliant future that they look forward to. This is the most perfect expression of all that the gift of love is capable of creating in our lives!

It is wonderful to embrace loving couples everywhere. How you describe yourselves to each other and the world and the gender of the love of your life may be very important to you.

Who will be walking down the aisle? That is up to you. You can both walk down the aisle if you desire. The father or fathers (or mothers or any other family member or friend) can escort their sons or daughters in together or separately. Civil weddings are wonderful in that they are flexible.

Attendant Titles

Bride/Groom: Spouse, Partner, Husband, Wife, Mate.

Bridesmaid/groomsman: Brides man, Grooms maid, Brides person, Grooms person, Best person, Person of Honour.

Best man/Maid of honour: Best person, Best woman, Best woman, Man of Honour, Person of Honor, Attendant of Honour

SAME SEX CEREMONY EXAMPLE 1

Welcome. Name and Name chose this beautiful site for their wedding because of their shared love of the country/beach.

The contract of marriage is one not to be entered into lightly, but thoughtfully and with a deep realisation of the obligations and responsibilities it entails. The commitment of marriage is different from all others. It is a lifelong bond that unites two people for better or for worse. Love, loyalty, and understanding are the foundation of a happy home. There are no human ties more important or more tender than marriage.

One of the great universals in human life across all boundaries and throughout the world is love. We see it in families and among friends. As young children in our mother's arms we are taught to value love in others. How wonderful it is to know people who have learned to value, honour and respect love. Today you are invited to celebrate love between two people. The love that binds them together and makes them one. May all who see this love be warmed by its joy.

SAME SEX CEREMONY EXAMPLE 2

Welcome! We are gathered here today to share in a celebration of love, and to join together forever the hearts of Name and Name. Today in the presence of family and friends, they will join their lives together. Two beautiful souls sharing the most sacred and tender of human relationships. They have invited us here today to rejoice, celebrate and bear witness to this sacred union. They stand before you bound by their love for each other, and the desire to share this expression of their love with you and with the world. We, their families and friends, form a community of love that together we may support and encourage them with our abundance of prayers and blessings on this day and for all of their lives.

BLESSING

At this time I ask that you join me in a blessing for Name and Name, as they begin the journey on their path of togetherness.

May life bless them and guide them on their journey together. Strengthening their kindness, compassion, trust and faith in each other. May their home be a haven for all who enter and their love be a constant example of the grace and beauty that the magic that is the gift of love embodies for all of us.

SAME SEX CEREMONY EXAMPLE 3

Family and friends, welcome with love. Today we unite to celebrate love! Love is perhaps the greatest gift that we can give each other. Love provides is the sustenance of life in that nourishes and fuels our souls. Love motivates us, brings joy to our hearts and truly gives us comfort. We can endure many things in this world but without being able to give, share and feel love our lives are unfulfilled. When we are able to give and receive the gift of love, our life becomes full of hope, of possibilities for love truly is life. Name and Name have made a commitment to each other to love, support, and share their life. Marriage is not merely a commitment to each other, but also a commitment to share their life with family and friends. Love becomes a community and the community today needs love. Today is about love and about celebrating love's purpose and its importance in our lives. Love gives us hope.

SAND CEREMONY

A *Sand Ceremony* or *Blending of the Sand* is a unique way to symbolise two lives becoming one. This is also a great way to incorporate children or family into the wedding ceremony.

There are varying styles of sand ceremony and relative wording. One style of the ceremony involves four containers. Three of which are filled with a different colours of sand. One colour symbolises the Bride, one the Groom, and the last symbolising family and friends of the couple in support of the marriage. The fourth container is a more elaborate keepsake into which the three containers of sand are poured. Firstly by the Bride, the Groom and the Celebrant (representing the family). Layering the coloured sands symbolically becomes a representation of the Bride and Groom as unique individuals. The blending of the sands then represents their two lives coming together as one.

Most ceremonies use glass containers such as a lovely vase or heart shaped bottle, to show off the blended colours of sand. If you prefer to use normal sand the container choice is unlimited. Coloured sand can be purchased in sealed bags.

A sand ceremony works particularly well when blending families, giving each child a role within the ceremony and highlighting his or her importance within the family unit.

Sand Ceremony to include in a Baby Naming:

BLENDING OF THE SANDS

Today (Couples names) have decided to have a blending of the sands. They have chosen sand that has been coloured like the colours of the rainbow, to signify that each of us is different and a valued and a special addition to the family. Everyone in the family has unique qualities and talents that make them the individuals they are.

Today, (Couples names) use colours to indicate the people in (Baby's) life. They have chosen the colours … for Mother, Father, Baby etc.

The blending of the sands will signify the blending of family. These sands will be mixed to indicate that once poured together no-one can return the sands to their individual state.

(Everyone pours the sand into the main jar)

The sand has now been joined together and cannot be isolated. They can never be separated and poured again into the individual containers.

Like colours of the rainbow, we're all different and special, valuable and precious. Each of us has unique qualities and talents which makes us the individuals we are.

Today, we use colours to indicate the people making up (Baby's) life. They stand for (Baby's) (Father), (Mother), (Baby's Sister) and (Baby).

When these sands are blended together, these four people join in their commitment to (Baby) and to each other becoming an united family unit.

(Everyone pours the sand into the main jar)

The sand has now been joined together and cannot be isolated. These grains of sand can never be separated and poured again into the individual containers, so will your family be a blending of four individual personalities, bonded together in a loving, supportive family unit.

Sand Ceremony 1

Bride and Groom, today you join your separate lives together. The two separate bottles of sand symbolise your separate lives, separate families and separate sets of friends. They represent all that you are and all that you will ever be as an individual. They also represent your lives before today.

As these two containers of sand are poured into the third container, the individual containers of sand will no longer exist, but will be joined together as one. Just as these grains of sand can never be separated and poured again into the individual containers, so will your marriage be.

Sand Ceremony 2

Bride and Groom, you have sealed your relationship by the giving and receiving of rings. This is your pledge to commit yourselves to one another throughout your lives.

Today, this relationship is also symbolised through the pouring of these two individual containers of sand. One, representing you Groom and one representing you Bride and all that you were, all that you are, and all that you will ever be.

As these two containers of sand are poured into the third container, the individual containers of sand will no longer exist, but will be joined together as one.

Just as these grains of sand can never be separated, our prayer for you today is that your lives together would be blended like the seven seas and may your love swirl around each other like the changing tides.

Sand Ceremony 3

Today, Bride and Groom have decided to use a Sand Ceremony to symbolise their relationship by pouring sand from these two individual containers of sand.

One container representing Groom and all that you were, all that you are, and all that you will ever be and the other representing you Bride and all that you were, all that you are, and all that you will ever be.

As these two containers of sand are poured into the third container, the individual containers of sand will no longer exist, but will be joined together as one. Just as these grains of sand can never be separated and poured again into the individual containers, may your marriage never be separated.

Sand Ceremony 4

Three colours of sand are layered in a vase to symbolise the importance of the individuals within the marriage and the joining of the two lives into one entity.

The sculpture begins with a layer of neutral sand to symbolize that the marriage is grounded.

The next layers are the individual colors representing the Bride and Groom which symbolizes that the foundation of the marriage is based on the strength of the individuals.

The final layer is the Bride and Groom's colors combined to symbolize the joining of their lives as one in marriage.

FAMILY SAND CEREMONY 5

Bride and Groom, today you are making a life-long commitment to share the rest of your lives with each other and honour your children as well.

Your family relationship is symbolized through the pouring of these individual containers of sand; one, representing you, BRIDE and all that you were, all that you are, and all that you will ever be, one representing you, GROOM, and all that you were and all that you are, and all that you will ever be and another container for each child.

There are children who will share in this marriage.

The gathering of this new family will have a deep influence upon them.

We realize that in order for the home to be a happy one, it is essential that there be love and understanding between the children and the adults being married.

As you each hold your sand the separate containers of sand represent your lives to this moment; individual and unique.

As you now combine your sand together, your lives also join together as one family.

You may now blend the sand together symbolizing the uniting of the children and Bride and Groom into one.

Just as these grains of sand can never be separated and poured again into the individual containers, so will your marriage and your family be.

Family Sand Ceremony 6

Four colors of sand are layered in a vase to symbolize the importance of the individuals within the marriage and the joining of the two lives into one entity.

The sculpture begins with a layer from each mother. This is to symbolize that the marriage is grounded by each of their families.

The next layers are the individual colors representing Bride and Groom, which symbolizes that the foundation of the marriage is based on the strength of each other as individuals.

The final layer is Bride and Groom's colors combined to symbolize the joining of their lives as one in marriage.

Family Sand Ceremony 7

Each of you in attendance this evening was asked to be here because you hold a special place in Groom's and Bride's life.

You came to honour and witness their love and commitment. GROOM and BRIDE wanted to make each of you a tangible part of this ceremony therefore, as each of you arrived this evening and entered into this scared space you were asked to spoon a small amount of white sand into a container.

They chose white sand because of the purity of your love and support to them and their family.

Bride and Groom have chosen varying shades of blue sand for themselves and for Children's names.

Each shade of blue represents each one of them.

These blues stand for the peace and calm they feel when together. It stands for the ocean waters deep and full of mystery and beauty.

Water that sustains all of life…

Water a great conductor of energy…

Water a simple element yet it can change and adapt to any form or environment.

At this time I ask you, Bride and Groom to pour some of your sand into the container because your marriage is the foundation of your family.

Now, I ask that (Children's names) join you in pouring their sand together with yours to create a beautiful flow of love and energy.

Lastly, I will fill the remainder of the container with more white sand.

This white sand stands for Universal Love…

A love that is eternal and never-ending.

(Family names) please hold hands.

I ask all in attendance to join me in a prayer of blessing upon this beautiful family.

Family Sand Ceremony 8

Bride and Groom, today you are making a life-long commitment to share the rest of your lives with each other.

Your relationship is symbolized through the pouring of these individual containers of sand; one, representing you, BRIDE and all that you were, all that you are, and all that you will ever be, and the other representing you, GROOM, and all that you were and all that you are, and all that you will ever be.

As you each hold your sand the separate containers of sand represent your lives to this moment; individual and unique. As you now combine your sand together, your lives also join together as one family.

At this time, I would invite the parents of Bride and Groom to come forward. These four vials of sand represent the Bride and Groom and each family.

You may now blend the sand together symbolizing the uniting of the two families into one.

Just as these grains of sand can never be separated and poured again into the individual containers, so will your marriage and your families be.

Family Sand Ceremony 9

Parents, today you are making a life-long commitment to share the rest of your lives with each other and honour your children as well.

Your family relationship is symbolized through the pouring of these individual containers of sand; one, representing each one of you, all that you are, and all that you will ever be.

There are children who will share in this marriage. The gathering of this new family will have a deep influence upon them.

We realize that in order for the home to be a happy one, it is essential that there be love and understanding between the children and the adults being married.

As you each hold your sand the separate containers of sand represent your lives to this moment; individual and unique.

As you now combine your sand together, your lives also join together as one family.

You may now blend the sand together symbolizing the uniting of the children and Groom/Bride and Groom/Bride into one.

Just as these grains of sand can never be separated and poured again into the individual containers, so will your marriage and your family be. With this marriage, these two families are joined.

To the children:

(Children's name/s) You are most special to Bride and Groom and they want to provide not only the basic needs, but a nurturing and loving environment in which each of you can find the confidence to reach the highest goals of your hearts, minds and spirits. Know that you may come to them when you are worried, sad or upset and they will do their best to give you help and love. This is their promise to you today given with love.

Sand Ceremony 10

NOTE: This ceremony can use coloured sands with an explanation of what each colour represents for the couple, the children etc., or the colours of the four seasons can be chosen with a reading regarding what the meaning of the seasons brings to the couple.

E.g. the blue sand represents the colour of the ocean and the sky. Blue is perceived as a constant in our lives and the collective colour of the spirit. May the colour blue invoke peace and calm in this marriage.

Celebrant: Like colours of the rainbow we're all different and special, valuable, and precious. Therefore it is only fitting that you be shown as an important part of this marriage, for marriage is really about family. These containers of sand represent each of you and your importance in this family. I will ask each of you to now pour some of your sand into the container. The sand has now been joined together and cannot be isolated. These grains of sand can never be separated and poured again into the individual containers, so will your family be a blending of 5 individual personalities, bonded together. You are joined together today, not only in marriage, but also as a family."

Celebrant: Groom and Bride, today you are making a commitment to share the rest of your lives with each other. Your relationship is symbolised through the pouring of these two individual containers of sand, one, representing you, Groom and all that you were, all that you are, and all that you will ever be, and the other representing you, Bride, and all that you were and all that you are, and all that you will ever be.

As you each hold your sand the separate containers of sand represent your lives to this moment, individual and unique. As you now combine your sand together, your lives also join together as one. You may now blend the sand together symbolising the uniting of your individual lives into one entity.

SAND CEREMONY 11

Today, this relationship is symbolised through the pouring of these different colours of sand. Each colour has been chosen for its special significance by Joe and Sue.

Joe has chosen the colour blue, for blue is the colour of intuition and communication which is most important in marriage. Sue has chosen the colour yellow. Yellow shines with optimism, enlightenment, and happiness. Yellow carries the promise of a positive future, and that is the dearest wish of Sue and Joe, a positive future for their married life together. As these two containers of sand are poured into the third container, the individual containers of sand will no longer exist, but will be joined together as one. When sand is blended the individual grains can never be separated back into the original containers. May Bride and Groom's marriage be as these grains of sand, unified and everlasting.

Sand Ceremony 12

Bride and Groom, you have just committed yourselves to one another through sacred vows. Your lives are no longer two, but one. To symbolise this joining, we ask that you each pour some sand into this bottle. (Each scoops some sand from the beach and pours it into the bottle).

Groom and Bride, as you pour your sand into the one container, please repeat after me: "As these grains of sand merge together as one, I merge my life with yours. Please take my love throughout the sands of time. My heart is forever in your keeping."

Sand Ceremony 13

Bride and Groom, as these grains of sand are joined together, so are your hearts, your bodies and your souls in marriage. Please repeat after me: "My beloved (Name) as these grains of sand are joined together, so are our hearts, our bodies and our souls. I offer myself as your husband/wife forever.

Sand ceremony of hands

In this ceremony I ask the Bride and Groom to bend down and pick up a handful of sand and then the Groom holding his hand over the Brides I ask them to release the sand together.

Bride and Groom will now take up a handful of sand. This sand has separate particles each uniting to make a beautiful beach where many come to find enjoyment and comfort. Bride and Groom will release their handful of sand in a moment blending the sand particles as a symbol of their lives blending together to build a beautiful life through the enjoyment of each other and the comfort that their love brings to their hearts.

SAND CEREMONY WITH CHILDREN

The (children's name/s) your mother (and father/partner's name) love you very much, and want you to know that you are and will always be a very important part of their lives. Will you please pour some sand into this glass container along with your good wishes? That would mean so much to them." (Parents then hug and kiss their children!)

Bride and Groom, your lives are now joined in the most sacred and joyous of unions. We pray that your life be blessed. In the immortal words of the poet mystic William Blake, together may you...

> *See a world in a grain of sand*
> *and heaven in a wild flower.*
> *Hold infinity in the palm of your hand*
> *and eternity in an hour.*

SEASHELL BLESSING CEREMONY

This ceremony is similar to the stone ceremony. People make a wish on a seashell and go to the water's edge to throw the shells into the ocean. I know people buy shells for their guests to make a wish upon. Having lived by the ocean I am very conscious of environmental issues. I prefer that a member of the wedding party of myself visit the beach before the ceremony and seek some small shells that are on the shoreline to place in a plastic bag and then in a box or basket on the day to allow guests to choose one. . This way you are not using shells foreign to the area. They do not need to be very large or even complete shells. It is more about the blessing. As long as there are some sort of small shell s along the beach line it can wait until the ceremony. To keep control of the ceremony depending on how many people are there. I sometimes ask that whilst the couple are signing the marriage certificate family and friends do the blessing. It is a good way to keep them entertained. Especially he children. I ask guests not to wander to far as I will be recalling them for the presentation as soon as the paperwork has been signed.

SHARING FIRST DRINK AS HUSBAND AND WIFE

The years of life are as a cup of wine poured out for you to drink. The cup of wine contains within it the sweet wine of happiness, joy, hopes and delight. The same cup, at times, holds the bitter wine of disappointment, sorrow, grief and despair. Those who drink deeply of life, invite the full range of experiences into their being.

This cup is symbolic of the pledges you have made to one another to share together the fullness of life. As you drink from this cup, you acknowledge to one another that your lives, until this moment, separate, have become one vessel into which all your sorrows and joys, all your hopes and fears, all your dreams and dreads, will be poured, and from which you will find mutual sustenance. Many days you will sit at the same table and eat and drink together. Drink now and may the cup of your lives be sweet and full to overflowing.

STONE CEREMONY

The Stone Ceremony is a great way of involving all your wedding guests at your wedding ceremony. Small, sometimes polished stones or pebbles are handed to the wedding guests and wedding party as they arrive at the ceremony. Shells can also be used if a beach wedding.

During the wedding ceremony the wedding guests and bridal party hold these stones and make a loving wish for the couple's life and future together.

Each stone represents a special wish that the couple can take with them to reflect on during their married life together. A good idea is to ask your wedding guests to write their name and a word signifying their wish on the stone, such as love, happiness, health, strength, wealth, success, family, luck, friendship, patience etc.

Just make sure that the pens you hand the guests to use are permanent and easy to write with. The stones are then collected during the wedding ceremony by a family or bridal party member and placed in a jar or vase as a memento.

SWEEPING THE BROOM

Delightfully the Bride and Groom have been swept off their feet by love. The tradition of Jumping the Broom symbolises sweeping away the old and welcoming the new. A symbol of a new beginning. The Bride and Groom sweep together in a circle to signify the sweeping away of their former single lives, any past problems and or previous cares.

TRADITIONAL CEREMONY

Dearly Beloved, We are gathered here together to join this man and this woman in Holy Matrimony. Who gives this Bride to be married to this Groom?

Her mother and I

We are gathered here today to celebrate one of life's greatest moments. To give recognition to the worth and beauty of love, which shall unite Groom's name and Bride's name in matrimony

Vows

Marriage is a partnership of two unique people who bring out the very best in each other and who know that even though they are wonderful as individuals, they are even better.

Groom, do you take Bride to be your wife? To live together in honour. To cherish her and keep her in sickness and in health for as long as you both shall live?

Bride, do you take Groom to be your husband? To live together in honour. To cherish him and keep him in sickness and in health for as long as you both shall live?

Ring Exchange

Wedding rings are an outward and visible sign of an inward spiritual grace, signifying to all the uniting of this man and this woman in marriage.

Groom, place the ring on Bride's finger and repeat after me.

I give you this ring, as a token and pledge, of my constant faith, and abiding love.

Bride, place the ring on Groom's finger and repeat after me. I give you this ring, as a token and pledge, of my constant faith, and abiding love.

By the authority vestedd in me and with the blessings of all present, I now pronounce you husband and wife. As the kiss is the messenger of the heart and soul, allow your souls to meet. You may kiss your lovely Bride.

Ladies and Gentlemen may I introduce to you Mr. & Mrs.

TREE CIRCLE (CAIRN)

The Cain is an early Celtic custom. At the start of ceremony the bride and groom draw a circle around themselves as a sign of their unity with God. As the circle is drawn the words, "The Mighty Tree, My protection be. Encircle me. My life, my love, my home. Encircle me. O sacred and mighty Tree. Your branches our shelter. Your wood our home. Soil to soil.

TREE PLANTING CEREMONY

Planting a wedding tree by a couple is an old custom with the belief that if the tree flourished and lived long, the marriage would be a happy one of long duration.

A marriage with the presence of trees, or planting of trees, was common in ancient Indian ceremonies for it is believed they bestow good times and are a messenger from earth to heaven. Trees and plants are worshipped and play important ritualistic roles. It is believed that spirits sit in the branches of trees.

A marriage with the presence of trees, or planting of trees, was common in ancient Indian ceremonies for it is believed they bestow good times and are a messenger from earth to heaven. Trees and plants are worshipped and play important ritualistic roles. It is believed that spirits sit in the branches of trees.

There are many variations on the tree planting ceremony and the style and wording can be adjusted to suit the ceremony.

Ancient civilizations thought trees to be sacred, connecting all forms of creation, a symbol of life. Like the tree, a happy marriage connects, creates and brings beauty to the world. A tree seed may travel great distances and grow sometimes in the face of adversity into a strong and beautiful canopy. The root system extends over large distances enriching, binding and supporting the earth. It provides not only material, but shade, food, and shelter. To grow healthy and strong a marriage must be like a tree. It also needs nourishment and support to survive. It must be carefully nurtured and protected to enable it to grow strong. Like timeworn timber, a marriage must be resilient to weather the challenges of life and the passage of time.

A tree may lose its leaves or blossom and be laid bare, yet it will burst into bloom again with the return of spring. So marriage at times may lose bloom, or be laid bare, yet through love and consideration, it too can survive the seasons. Over time things change, but the essence of a loving marriage will remain, strong yet flexible, rooted deep into the earth of family life.

After the ceremony, Bride and Groom will take this potted tree/plant, and transplant it at their home to symbolise putting down roots, longevity and strength within their marriage.

TREE PLANTING CEREMONY

Bride and Groom will plant this tree as an affirmation of their lifelong love, with the promise to care for it. Caring for their tree will be a daily reminder to also nurture and nourish their marriage with encouragement, consideration and companionship.

TYING OF THE KNOT

(ANOTHER HAND FASTING EXAMPLE)

The tying of hands is a centuries old custom. The two separate ends looped over into a knot represent two becoming one. To tie means to "bind." The knot means to secure, so when you tie the knot you are symbolically bonding and securing the marriage. Over time variations of this tradition have evolved and are still evolving.

Hand fasting is a betrothal or wedding ritual in which the couple's clasped hands are tied together by a cord or ribbon — hence the phrase "tying the knot". The modern hand fasting ritual typically consists of tying the right hands of the couple to be betrothed, or wed with a ribbon or cord while the couples exchange their vows or after they exchange their vows. Historically, the ritual was done during the time of the Roman Empire and more ancient times. In Ireland and Scotland, during the early Christian period it was a form of trial marriage, often performed in rural areas when a priest was not available. The couple could form a temporary, trial marriage, and then be married "in the Church" the next time a priest visited their area.

The mothers of the Bride and Groom present the Bride and Groom with a piece of ribbon of different colours. The Celebrant says a few words about the knots being individual and separate until the Bride and Groom make them one with a knot. The Bride and Groom then tie the ribbons in a knot.

e.g.

Bride and Groom, since your lives have crossed in this life, you have formed ties between each other. In entering marriage, you have agreed to work to give meaning both to this ceremony and your relationship. Within this circle, you are not only declaring before family and friends that you are binding yourself together in life.

OR

Bride and Groom clasp hands. We will now bind your hands with this cord, just as your love and your vows shall bind you fast together. We tie a knot to symbolise the circle of infinity and lasting love. As your hands are joined so if your life joined. (Hands tied with loose knot). In order to bring forth the best of yourselves you must engage your full measure of energy and passion so that your life together is filled with both. I give my blessings to this binding.

Using Coloured Ribbons

White: This represents the white strand of life. It is newness and beginnings, purity and innocence. All things have a youth. Cherish the youth of your bodies and relationships, understanding that they will change as time passes. Whether those changes are for the better, or for the worse, are up to you.

Red: This represents the red strand of life. It is progress and fertility, strength, determination and maturity. All things mature in time. Cherish the fullness of life, and the achievements for which you work so hard, understanding that the road to maturity has many twists and turns. Whether you dislike the person you are when you reach the summit, is up to you.

Black: This represents the black strand of life. It is age, wisdom and experience. All things age and die. Cherish the hard won knowledge and memories of your journey through time, understanding that they are keys to the universe. Whether you decide to use them to make the world a better place is up to you.

Green: This represents the green strand of life. It is action and interaction, communication and generosity in your partnership. All things interact with their surroundings. Cherish the dance of your similarities and differences, understanding that as you each grow and change, so will your dances. Whether your dance continues to bring you joy is up to you.

Brown/Blue/Yellow

And finally the three strands of the physical world together as one, binding their lives in reality.

This is the *brown* strand of line. It is the earth.

This is the *blue* strand of life. It is the waters.

This is the *yellow* strand of life. It is the sun.

These are the foundations of life, from which all life springs and on which all life is dependant.

Vow

Just as your vows are binding, so is this knot. Keep it to ever remind you of your spiritual union. Treasure and keep it intact as you marriage should be nurtured, so it too remains tied with the intricacy of love and respect.

Presentation

Ladies and Gentlemen, Bride and Groom have declared before us their desire to share their lives in marriage. They have made this commitment through sincere promises made to each other in this their special ceremony. In an ancient tradition they have symbolised their union by being bound together, taking vows and exchanging rings. It is therefore my pleasure and an honour to declare Bride and Groom to be husband and wife.

UNITY BOWL RITUAL

This tradition is a way to honour multiple generations of the Bride and Groom's families, and/or a way to include any children that the couple may have. This is one example and can be varied:

The couple selects a glass bowl they would enjoy having in their new home. Each grandparent, parent, stepparent, godparent and so on is given a small lovely container filled with a different colour of flat glass marbles, sand etc. with the separate colours signifying the individuality of each family member. Colours can be chosen to match the wedding ceremony, or a beautiful reading can be read out as each colour is added to the bowl signifying what the colour represents to the couple e.g.

"Blue is the colour of the sky and represents inspiration, sincerity and spirituality. This calming and soothing colour epitomizes the serenity and peace that love has brought to Bride and Groom."

The grandparents pour their separate colours into the Unity Bowl as the foundation of the wedding of the Bride and Groom. Each set of parents does the same. Then the Bride and Groom add their two colours. If there are children, they add theirs after the Bride and Groom. Siblings and other special friends may be invited to participate, as well. Ultimately, the family members are reminded that each of them, in their own way, has coloured the lives of the Bride and Groom. Therefore, each has developed individual tastes, goals, morals, and choices.

Finally, it is noted that, just as the colours have blended to make a mosaic and changed the design as they are blended, so is change the most dependable constant in the couple's married life. They are called on to embrace change, be flexible and grow with each change.

Thus they get to keep a memento placed in their Unity Bowl by all the family members and other loved ones who were present at their wedding. An emotional reminder that changes can be beautiful, as long as they keep the right perspective, they will adapt and learn from change.

VOW WITH CHILDREN

Vow with Children 1

I have pledged my love to you and I want to add a vow to the children. I promise to treat (children's names) with respect, consideration and love. I gladly accept the obligations that go along with this pledge and acknowledge them as part of my life.

(Children's names) as you grow and become young men and women in your own right, we will do our best to always be there for you. We will love you and open ourselves to your questions and your needs, so that you feel safe and secure in our love for you.

Vow with Children 2

As a symbol of this pledge, a gift of love and unity is presented to each child during the ceremony. Children step forward and receive their gift.

WARMING OF THE RINGS

During this ceremony Groom and Bride will exchange rings. They have entrusted the keeping of the rings with (person's name). These rings are the visible signs of their commitment to one another. As this ceremony proceeds we ask that the families of Groom and Bride take part in the warming of the rings.

We ask that you, their family and friends wish them health and happiness, and all that is noble and good in life. (Person's name) will now pass these rings to the families of Groom and Bride and I ask that each family member hold them for a moment, warm them with your love, then pass them on to the next person. I ask that all present voice a silent wish or prayer for this couple, for their marriage and their future together.

When these rings come back to (person's name) they will contain in their precious metal, that which is more precious, that which is priceless, your love and hope and pledge of support for this union. (Music played while the rings are being warmed)

OR

Bride and Groom will be wearing rings as a sign of their commitment to one another. As we proceed with the ceremony, their rings will be passed to each of you with the invitation family and friends, to take part in the warming of the rings by holding them for a moment to warm them with your love. We ask that you make a silent wish for this couple and their future together. When these rings come back they will contain in their precious metal, that which is more precious, that which is priceless, our love and hope and pledge of support for their marriage. (The rings make their way around to each of the guests, as the ceremony proceeds)

WEDDING CUSTOMS FROM AROUND THE WORLD

At the library and on the internet you will find extracts from ritual, religious, spiritual, Hindu, Buddhist, as well as non-traditional and traditional rituals and ceremonies.

There are also poems, reading, quotes etc. There are many variations that will assist your personal choice in taking your ceremony to a very personal level.

WINE – SHARING OF WINE (QUAICH)

A two handled cup was traditionally used during wedding feasts to symbolise sharing between the newly wedded couple. Presented using both hands, the recipient must receive it with both hands. Continuing the tradition, the Quaich is still serving its purpose today, uniting friends and the two families in the Celtic wedding ceremony.

The goblet of wine is symbolic of the cup of life. "As you share this wine, you promise to share all that the future will bring. The sweetness the cup of life holds for you is sweeter because you drink it together and whatever drops of bitterness it contains are less because they are shared." Bride and Groom sip from goblet.

In a Jewish ceremony the Bride and Groom drink from a single glass of wine. This symbolizes drinking from the cup of life and sharing all of its experiences together, both bitter and sweet. After drinking the glass is placed in a velvet bag and crushed underfoot by the Groom. As the glass is broken so is the couple irrevocably tied.

WINE CEREMONY 1

This glass of wine symbolizes the sum of your life experiences. It contains within it the sweet flavors of love, joy, wonder and contentment.

As you drink from this cup, you accept the commitment to draw from your marriage all that you need to savour the sweet flavours you may encounter on your journey together.

Wine Ceremony 2

As you have shared wine from a single cup, so may you be blessed that under life's guidance you will share contentment, peace and fulfillment from the cup of life.

May you find life's joys heightened, its bitterness sweetened, and each of its moments hallowed by true companionship and love?

Wine Ceremony 3

Life is a series of contradictions. It is said that all things end and yet all things continue. Wine has been called the symbol of life like the blood flowing within our bodies. By sharing this glass, two become one, the parts become whole; two paths intertwined and united in love. As you share this wine glass today, may you be joined in a love as fluid as the drink itself, with a marriage as solid as the hands that made it.

Wine Ceremony 4

This wine glass is to remind you of your love. Delicate, yet strong; filled with love, yet with room for more. Use this loving cup for miracles. Drink deeply of forgiveness, understanding and appreciation. Real love once created, cannot be destroyed.

Wine Ceremony 5

May this cup serve as a ceremonial loving cup for your relationship. In this glass are the fruits of God, Mankind and Mother Earth. The years of your lives are like a cup of wine that is poured out for the sake of labour, honour and love. Many days you will sit at the same table and eat and drink together. Many are the experiences you will share. As with a glass of wine, one of you may find it sweet, the other perhaps dry or somehow different. Let the drink you share today serve as a reminder that although you may perceive things very differently, being right is never more important than being happy.

With this space that you give each other, always putting your commitment to love and honour one another first, your lives together will grow deeper, richer and greatly satisfying, like a rare and fine wine. You may now drink from this fountain of love.

WINE CEREMONY 6

Kahlil Gibran writes in "the Prophet":

> Love one another, but make not a bond of love. Let it rather be a moving sea between the shores of your souls. Fill each other's cup, but drink not from one cup.

(Groom fills glass with wine) Fill each other's cup but drink from your own.

Let this symbolize your promise to each other to be yourselves to the fullest and at the same time to honour the unity you share as husband and wife and to cherish the gifts of love and nurturing each gives the other.

I invite you now to drink to one another . . . Let this drinking of wine also remind you that what matters most in life is the spirit, not the letter; the wine, not the cup.

Wine Ceremony 7

Like wine, life is a process of change and nurturing. As grapes are pressed to give forth their juice, so under the press of time our lives give forth their labour, honour and love. Long ago, wine was revered as the blood of the earth from which comes sustenance.

When the Bride and Groom pledged themselves to one another, they drank wine from a single cup, signifying that they were becoming one blood, one family.

The sharing of wine a reminder that a good wine is only enjoyed if it is savoured when consumed. So must life be savored when consumed until the last drop.

Wine Ceremony 8

Bride and Groom, this "Cup of Life" contains within it a wine with certain properties that are sweet and symbolic of happiness, joy, ecstasy and love just as the years of life ahead of you together will be. This same wine also holds some bitter properties that symbolise disappointment, sorrow, grief, despair, and life's trials and tribulations that you will inevitably run into during your new life together.

Forgive the frailties of one another's flaws, for they will be overcome and bear life's adversities with the confidence that the strength of your love will always prevail.

Drink from this cup together the first toast of your union. May pleasure and prosperity may come to you with gratitude and modesty.

WINE CEREMONY 9

The sweetness and the bitterness of this wine as it has matured represents life's many ups and downs, some sweet, some bitter .

Those who drink deeply from the "Cup of Life" with an open heart and willing spirit, invite the full range of challenges and experiences into their being.

This "Cup of Life" is symbolic of the pledges you have made to one another this evening, to share together the fullness of life. As you drink from this cup, you acknowledge to one another that your lives until this moment separate have now become one. Drink now, and may the cup of your lives be overflowing!

WINE CEREMONY 10

As you have shared this cup of wine, so may you share your lives. May all the sweetness that life holds for you be that much sweeter because you taste it together.

May you find life's joys heightened, its bitterness sweetened and your life enriched by a constant love. As you share the wine from this cup, so may you share your lives. May this bond that ties you hold forever true! Please share this cup of wine one last time as an acknowledgment of the new bond between you as life partners, soul mates, husband and wife.

WINE CEREMONY 11

The years of life are like a cup of wine. This wine contains certain properties that are sweet and symbolic of happiness, joy, hope, peace, love and delight.

The same wine also holds a tint of bitter properties that are symbolic of disappointment, sorrow, grief, despair, and life's trials and tribulations. Together the sweet and the bitter represent "Love's Journey" and all of the experiences that are a natural part of it.

(Celebrant pours wine into the cup and holds it up)

This cup of wine is symbolic of the cup of life. When you drink deeply of this cup you invite the full spectrum of experiences into your life. You accept the commitment to draw from your marriage all that you need to. Savouring the sweet and swallowing any bitter flavours of life you will experience on your journey together.

This cup is also symbolic of the pledges you have made to one another to share together the fullness of life. To acknowledge to one another that your lives, separate until this moment, have now become one.

(Celebrant hands the cup to Bride and Groom)

Now drink to the love you've shared in the past.

(The Bride and Groom sip from the cup.)

Drink to your love in the present on this you're wedding day.

(The Bride and Groom sip from the cup.)

And drink to your love in the future and forever more!

(The Bride and Groom sip from the cup and hand it back to the Celebrant.)

As you have shared the wine from this cup, so may you share your lives.

May you explore the mysteries of life in the reflection of your love.

From love all things proceed and unto love they must return.

May you find your life enriched by blessings.

WINE CEREMONY 12

Life is a series of contradictions. It is said that all things end and yet all things continue. All things change and yet all things remain the same.

Wine has been called the symbol of life. It is like the blood flowing within our bodies. By sharing this glass, you symbolise the sharing of life. Two become one, the parts become whole; two paths intertwined, each separate, yet united in love.

WINE CEREMONY 13

The years of our lives are as a cup of wine. Grapes when they are pressed give forth their juices for the wine. Life also pressed gives out the juices of its labour. Bride and Groom, often in the days to come you will share bread and wine the cup of life.

Drink now, and may the cup of your lives be sweet and full to running over. As you have shared from this one cup of wine, so may you draw contentment, comfort, and delight from the cup of life. May you find life's joys heightened, its bitterness sweetened, and all things hallowed, by your companionship and love.

WINE CEREMONY 14

This Ceremony represents the two individual lives which are now combined like the two wines into one single cup. The drinking of the combined wine signifies the commitment you now make to live your lives as one family. Today you seal with the drinking wine the joining your lives as one.

WINE CEREMONY 15

We Now Shall Perform the Wine Ceremony.

The couple goes to the table and each takes the individual carafe and pours some wine into the larger carafe. The Groom then takes the larger filled carafe with the combined wine and pours some in a glass for the Bride. The Bride then takes the Larger Carafe with the combined wines and pours some into a glass for the Groom. He may now toast his Bride with, "Now Our Lives Are One" and drinks from the glass she responds the same. They place the wine glass back and face back to the Celebrant.)

This Ceremony represents the two individual lives are now combined like the two wines into one single life. The drinking of the combined wine signifies the commitment you now make to live your lives as one family. May you remember this day of commitment you have sealed with drinking of the new wine joining your lives as one.

Family Wine Ceremony 16

Wine is a universal symbol of the richness of life and sweetness of love. It is appropriate that on this joyous occasion Bride and Groom toast their marriage for the first time with this ancient symbolism.

(Parents), please fill your carafes. (Each set parents pours wine into a carafe)

This wine represents the continuous connection between these parents. It is symbolic of the love and encouragement you have provided your child and will continue to provide them in their lives.

Bride's parents come forth and pour wine into carafe. Grooms parents come forth and pour wine into carafe. Wife is poured into Bride and Grooms glasses.

Now Bride and Groom drink from each other's cups as a sign of sharing yourselves and your life together. (Drink)

Let this wine ceremony represent the spirit of your lives together. By sharing this wine you bless the unity of yourself and your families.

WITH US IN SPIRIT

Those With Us in Spirit allows a moment to remember those who have passed away.

THOSE WITH US IN SPIRIT 1

At this time, we'd like to take a moment of silence to remember those who are not here with us. Even though they are not here physically, they are a part of the foundation that makes Bride and Groom the people they are today.

May we always remember (names of those who passed). Please cherish the memories of these friends and family and all others who live on in our hearts. Amen.

THOSE WITH US IN SPIRIT 2

We would like to take a moment to recognize those that could not be here today. While they may not physically be with us, Bride and Groom feel their love and support.

THOSE WITH US IN SPIRIT 3

We now close our eyes and bring to mind any loved ones who could not be here today. Though they are absent physically, we invoke, through our thought and prayers, their loving presence.

We pray that God might multiply beyond measure the blessings from these loved ones to this loving couple, and any children who might one day be a part of this union. Now, from our hearts, we ourselves visualize and sanctify all the blessings we would bestow on Bride and Groom in their lives as a couple and a family. And in our sincere desire to bless, we in turn, are blessed also. Blessed Be.

The Service

Modern weddings are much more casual and creative today with the opportunity of choosing to have a Civil marriage ceremony. This type of ceremony gives you the opportunity to incorporate your personality into the ceremony.

The wedding script is the heart of the wedding ceremony

The elements of a wedding script are as follows and not necessarily in this order. No. 4 The Monitum and No. 5 the Legal Vows must be included as a legal requirement.

1. Introduction/Welcome

2. Reading, poem and/or prayer *(Only if desired)*

3. **Monitum**

4. Questions of intent ("Will you have this man/woman?) *(Only if desired)*

5. **Legal Vows**

6. Personal Vows *(Only if desired)*

7. Reading, poem and/or prayer *(Only if desired)*

8. Pronouncement as husband and wife

9. Presentation of couple, Mr. and Mrs.……

VENUE

Remember to check when you book your venue regarding any restrictions, notifications, or fees that need to be paid, which may be the case if you have your wedding in a park, garden, or on the beach.

Don't forget to factor in the weather and consider an alternative venue if the weather changes. Is parking available and access for older guests? Who is going to be responsible for the music at the ceremony? Is power required?

Consider including a map with the wedding invitations and instructions where to meet, as well as information about an alternate venue, if there is inclement weather.

WEARING THE KILT/TARTAN

One of the most unique ways to bring the spirit of the Celts into your wedding is to have the men and boys in the wedding party dress in kilts. The full formal kilt attire consists of a tartan kilt, Prince Charlie Jacket and vest, fur or leather sporran, kilt socks and flashes, and any dress shoes.

A tuxedo shirt and black bow tie are worn but a less formal button-down shirt with a tweed jacket or an Argyll jacket with tartan tie is appropriate. Additional items are kilt belts and sgian dubh, a small knife with or without a sheath worn slipped into the top of the kilt sock.

Scottish Wedding Prayer

Lord help us to remember when we first met and the
    strong
love that grew between us. To work that love into
practical things so that nothing can divide us.
We ask for words both kind and loving and hearts always
ready to ask forgiveness as well as to forgive.

Old Marriage Song

Marry when the year is new, always loving, kind, and true.
When February birds do mate, you may wed, nor dread
    your fate.

If you wed when March winds blow, joy and sorrow both
    you'll know.
Marry in April when you can, joy for maiden and for
    man.

Marry in the month of May; you will surely rue the day.
Marry when June roses blow, over land and sea you'll go.

They who in July do wed, must labor always for their bread.
Whoever wed in August be, many a change are sure to see.

Marry in September's shine, your living will be rich and fine.
If in October you do marry, love will come but riches tarry.

If you wed in bleak November, only joy will come, remember.
When December's rain fall fast, marry and true love will last.

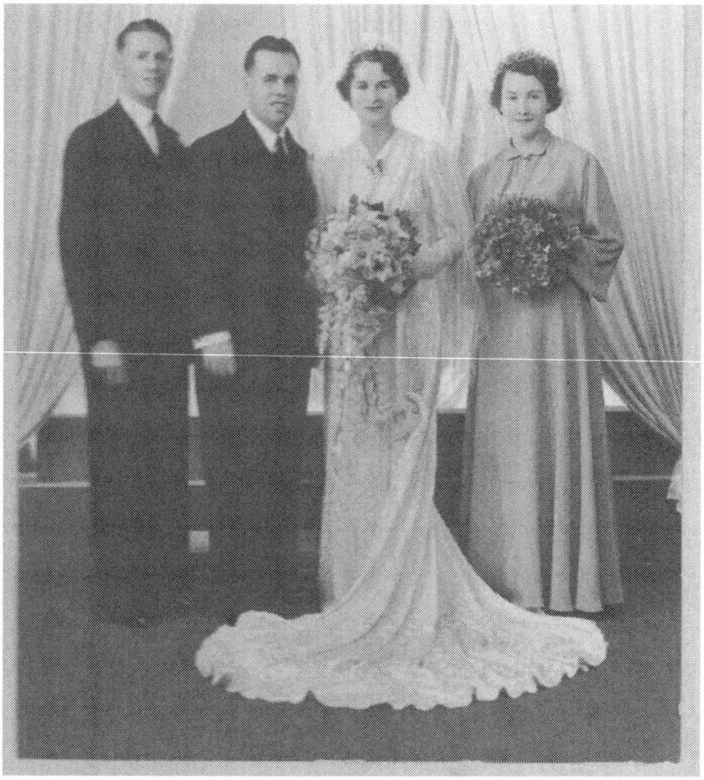

A–Z Index

B
Baby naming ceremony candle 7
Beach ceremony 18
Blended family ceremony 20
Blessing of the elements 22
Blessing of the hands 30
Blessing of the rings ceremony 32
Breaking the glass ceremony 39
Buddhist ceremony 44
Burning bowl ceremony 47
Butterfly release 49

C
Cairn. *See* Tree circle
Candle lighting unity ceremony 52
Celtic ring warming 59
Children's candle 61
Christian ceremony 64
Coin or arras ceremony 68
Commitment ceremony 66

D
Dove release 70

F
Family blessings 76
Family medallion 78
Family unity candle ceremony – children 80

G
Giving away the bride 82
Giving flowers to mothers of the bride and groom 84

H
Hand fasting 88
Hindu ceremony 105

J
Jumping the broom 108

K
Knot tying ceremony 111

L
Love letter ceremony 114

M
Marriage bell 119
Medieval ceremony 134
Memory candle 121

O
Oathing stone 123

Q
Quaich. *See* Sharing of wine

R
Ribbon ceremony 135
Ring warming ceremony 136
Rose ceremony 126, 139

S
Same sex ceremony 144
Sand ceremony 148
Sharing first drink as husband and wife 162
Sharing of wine 179
Stone ceremony 163
Sweeping the broom 164

T
Traditional ceremony 164
Tree circle 166
Tree planting ceremony 166
Tying of the knot 169

U
Unity bowl ritual 173

V
Vow with children 175

W
Warming of the rings 176
Wearing the kilt/tartan 191
Wedding customs from around the world 178
With us in spirit 188

Printed in Great Britain
by Amazon